Computers
and Teacher Training:
A Practical Guide

Computers
and Teacher Training:
A Practical Guide

Dennis M. Adams

University of Northern Colorado, Greeley

The Haworth Press
New York • London

Computers and Teacher Training: A Practical Guide is monographic supplement #1 to the journal *Computers in the Schools*, Volume 2, 1985. It is not supplied as part of the subscription to the journal, but is available from the publisher at an additional charge.

The Haworth Press, Inc., 12 West 32 Street, New York, New York 10001
EUROSPAN/Haworth, 3 Henrietta Street, London WC2E 8LU England

Library of Congress Cataloging in Publication Data

Adams, Dennis M.
    Computers and teacher training.

    "A Monographic supplement to the journal Computers in the schools, volume 2, 1985"—T.p. verso.
    Bibliography: p.
    1. Education—Data processing. 2. Computer-assisted instruction. 3. Computer literacy. 4. Education—Data processing—Social aspects. I. Computers in the schools. V. 2. (Supplement) II. Title.
LB1028.43.A33   1985   371.3'9445   85-16392
ISBN 0-86656-312-1
ISBN 0-86656-378-4 (pbk.)

Contents

Acknowledgments

I would like to acknowledge the important assistance of Deborah Bott and Mary L. Johnson, with contributions by Carolyn Keefe, Deborah Resnick, and Catherine Baird, David B. Thomas, Mary Fuchs, and John Cooney.

Computers
and Teacher Training:
A Practical Guide

Introduction

In teacher training we must be aware of a technological inno- vation as important as the computer. Being computer literate may become as important as being literate in the more traditional sense. Without this skill, we are excluded from many experiences and events. Familiarity with both the theory and potential applications of computers is essential. These machines can be a liberating force in education, empowering a new generation of adepts. This book focuses on how this computer-based technology can be used in the learning process. Its purpose is to help both those training to become teachers and teachers already in the field become familiar with a new technology that promises to leave a lasting imprint on the practice of education.

Report after report has cited the educational mediocrity in the country. The public is paying a great deal of attention to issues of efficiency and relevancy within education. With computers and computer-assisted activities penetrating every aspect of our lives, computers are definitely a relevant topic for education. And teaching effectiveness can be improved by using the technology to engage students in a more active process of thinking and problem solving.

As *Computers and Teacher Training* is an idea book, no attempt is made to take the traditional academic approach of citing case study after case study. Still, the need to relate theory and research to actual educational practice involving these intelligent machines is never forgotten. Both the experienced computing teacher and someone who has never touched a computer can use many things herein—in and outside of the classroom. Everything from what to look for in educational software to specific "off line" activities are provided. The idea is to help teachers tap computer-related technologies in ways that positively influence what is occurring in the classroom. Computers have now reached

1

a stage where they can bring us some magic. Let's take what they have to offer.

This book provides a structure for training and a success cycle of practice, proficiency, and pleasure. The framework is designed to assist teachers at all levels in learning about educational computing, computer-based telecommunications, artificial intelligence, and computer-related social issues. The focus is on self-development and faculty training faculty in a collegial and informational manner. In teacher training groups we frequently ask "What would you like to teach?", "What would you like to learn?" and "What impact might these machines (computers) have on the nature and effectiveness of education?"

Key concepts are set up for both independent and group work. Ideas are arranged in a manner that allows a teacher operating independently, a peer workshop leader, or college-level instructor to structure computer learning. Graphic displays and charted information have been added simply to enhance your understanding of the subject matter; however, many could be easily adapted as overhead transparencies.

For schools, it is always a good idea to have an in-house expert—yet, there are many "functions" that require "input" from someone outside. No matter who is involved, the acquisition of computer competence should be viewed as developmental—a process of progressive learning for teachers.

Drawing on personal experiences and those of workshop leaders, the emphasis of this book is on *meaning*. Societal issues with regard to educational computing are discussed, and ideas for using both hardware and software are provided. An attempt is made to answer the question: "What kind of innovation is feasible and not prohibitively expensive?" The future direction that computer technology may take is evaluated so that teachers can prepare for an ever-changing technological world.

All the disciplines that make up the base of education are shifting. Hopefully, this book will serve as a resource for what students and teachers need to learn about the technological;

literacy-intensive environment of the future. A wider range of intellectual concerns will be needed: science/technology, the arts, and language. The result will be a new view of the liberal arts, with the fine arts interweaving with computer-based technology.

The intent of this book is to aid teachers in coping with the powerful forces that are shaping our future. As teachers, we need to be concerned with the connections between the two new basics—computing (the force here) and the humanities. The liberal arts will give us both the intellectual tools and an understanding of what we are teaching and why. The characteristics of effective instruction lead us to use art, drama, music, and literature as a bridge to the physical sciences and technology. The most successful educational programs build on the elements of challenge, fantasy, and curiosity in the process of integrating technology and the arts. Even our newest computers, like the Apple Macintosh, make heavy use of visual imagery. As science and computer-controlled technology change the very nature of knowledge and instruction, we need to be critically informed—not about a movement of the moment but about a tool that will help us dramatically expand the nature of instruction in all areas.

The very concept of knowledge itself may change as a result of the development of artificial intelligence which can be used to assist human reasoning activity. Putting knowledge processing to work in computers will be of major importance. Why? Because most of the information processing attending the world's work involves reasoning and problem solving. Numerical calculation and data processing may have been central to the first computer revolution; however, it is putting knowledge to work and communications that are central to the second. And it is this second computer revolution that is of critical importance to educators.

For the future, some researchers even envision machines that will run on something called a ''biochip,'' a half-living, half-electronics cell. On a more immediate level, new computers are being developed that are dynamic, ever-changing repositories of knowledge that can be updated and changed through new experience. There is no question that the development of computer-based technology is an important intellectual development. Researchers are now in the process of finding ways to teach computers to draw inferences, make decisions, reach conclusions, recognize objects, read printed material, understand speech, and learn from experience. Aesthetic comprehension, effective thinking, communicating thought, making relevant judgments, and the ability to discriminate among conflicting values will become increasingly important in schooling as humans strive to employ these new tools.

Broadening perspectives and balancing the liberal arts, professional education, and technology are keys in helping teachers learn about computing. This book will get you off to a good start in considering the educational possibilities of computers and in enhancing your understanding and participation. It will also go a long way toward helping your exploration of the advantages and disadvantages that technology brings to the quality of life in our schools. We really are pioneers in a new technological era in education and the first scouting parties are just reporting back.

Chapter 1

A Look Back—A Look Ahead

By looking at how people in the past predicted the technological future, we can see where they were right and wrong. The past can help us do a better job of predicting the future. Tomorrow is not simply an enlarged today.

If we are to help our students understand what computers are and what they can become, it is helpful to look at the history of computers—from the abacus to the Apple. In this chapter, we look at how and why individuals built computing machines. We look ahead to the computers of the future and how they may change the lives of our students.

HOW LONG HAVE COMPUTERS BEEN WITH US?

Analog computers (like the slide rule), which operate by measuring the relationship between different lengths that represent different numbers, have been around since the dawn of civilization. Other mechanical aids to computation developed by the Egyptians, Greeks, Romans, and Chinese have been with us for thousands of years. The first digital computer, the abacus, was part of ancient culture; and this method of sliding beads back and forth has continued to be used by the Chinese to this day. Only recently have computers become faster than a man with an abacus. The computer revolution is already making many of our thinking skills obsolete. Historically, this is similar to the Industrial Revolution, which made certain thinking skills requiring muscle power obsolete.

In the seventeenth century Blaise Pascal came up with a calculating machine to help his father count the French census. Leibniz also developed a similar machine and drew up plans for a calculator that used a binary code.

Babbage's difference engine was inspired by the Jacquard loom, which programmed weaving by pulling threads through punched cards arranged to produce a pattern design. Seventy years later, the same 80-vertical-column punch cards were used by IBM. Unlike most mechanical tools (the typewriter, for example), there is no "inventor" of the computer. Charles Babbage is about as close as we can come. Working in England in the early 1820s, he devised the difference engine—a machine for computing algebraic problems. Based on his successful pilot project, he applied to the Chancellor of the Exchequer for funds to build a large, steam-generated computational device. Although it worked, the available power source—steam—did not allow it to operate quickly enough to significantly change the nature of computation.

Babbage made some of the same mistakes we are making today. He did not know what problems he wanted to solve. He did not develop any programs, and he came to rely on one machinist to run his machine. When he lost that key person, Lady Ada Lovelace, the whole project fell apart.

Babbage did come up with some positive lessons for today. For one thing, he made his programs and variables as general as possible—making optimum use of memory space. People—and present computers—go through the same five steps as Babbage's analytical engine to solve a problem: input, storage, control, calculation, and output. Although Babbage used 10 digits, it was not until the 1950s that we had computers that used the binary code of two digits that were, conceptually, a match for Babbage's engine.

Herman Hollerith, another early pioneer in computing, used electricity to develop a mechanical device to tabulate the 1890 census. That device, called the Hollerith card, used a series of punched holes to indicate age, sex, occupation, and so on. The cards went under contact brushes that completed an electrical circuit when there was a hole present and the cards were dropped into the appropriate bin. Hollerith even developed a card-punch machine and sorter. In the 1890s he founded the Tabulating Machine Company, which later became IBM. Hollerith's conceptual design formed the basis of IBM's business until 1960.

COMPUTERS IN EUROPE:
MOVING IN FITS AND STARTS TOWARD
WORLD WAR II

In Germany during the 1930s a young engineer, Konrad Zuse, spread out electronics parts and something like an erector set in his parents' living room. Zuse hated structured environments and liked to teach himself by playing with various components. The result was a computer that used telephone relays and a binary system of numbers. Zuse's design was taken and used by the Luftwaffe to calculate wing designs and later to figure the trajectory of the V-I rockets that rained down on England in 1944.

In England, during the 1930s, Alan Turing (who had visited Germany) was "playing with" electronic parts and philosophical concepts while studying at Cambridge. He developed a test for artificial intelligence: If a human being could not distinguish between human and machine response, then the machine was "intelligent." He also developed a primitive robot that could respond to its environment and even plug itself in when its batteries ran low.

In the late 1930s and early 1940s Turing was working on "Collossus," a computer that was very advanced for its time. He was given a clear strategic mission by the English government—to break the German military code. He did. And Churchill, Turing, and a few others knew what the Germans were going to do. This proved a strain on Turing because he knew, for example, that Coventry was going to be bombed twenty-four hours before the German attack. But since he could not give away the fact that he had broken the code (which was the only possibility for knowing about the raid), no warning was given and thousands died. Eccentric to begin with, Turing went mad after the war. In an imitation of Snow White, he ate a poisoned apple and died.

AMERICAN CANDIDATES FOR "INVENTOR OF THE ELECTRONIC DIGITAL COMPUTER"

The English or the Germans are sometimes credited with the real computer breakthroughs in the 1930s. However, in the United States we have at least three candidates for "inventor of the electronic digital computer." John Atanasoff is one. After working toward his Ph.D. in theoretical physics at the University of Wisconsin, Atanasoff took a teaching post at Iowa State College. Like most physicists at the time, he was interested in solving long, time-consuming problems with many variables. He knew something about the work of Leibniz, Pascal, and Babbage. Although he thought people would have more trouble understanding the binary system, he knew that using ones and zeros would be cheaper than using the ten digits of the decimal system. With a state research grant of $650, he bought materials, hired a graduate student (Clifford Berry), and started using vacuum tube devices for calculating. By 1940 he and Berry had developed the Atanasoff-Berry Computer, known as A.B.C. Programs were actually soldered into the A.B.C., and instructions could not be changed for solving a problem without resoldering.

John Mauchly at the Carnegie Institute in Washington had been working along similar lines. He realized that it would take many lifetimes to do the necessary calculations to figure some of his problems in atmospheric electricity, in spite of the large number of graduate students that he had hired at fifty cents an hour. Although there is some dispute as to who gave whom what, Mauchly and Atanasoff met during the development process and shared ideas.

During World War II, Mauchly met J. Presper Eckert at the University of Pennsylvania. For years, military researchers had been considering using vacuum tubes for computing. But Mauchly and Eckert were among the first to actually use them. The result was the ENIAC (Electronic Numerical Integrator and Calculator) computer (which is now on display at the Smithsonian).

However, it was not until the arrival of John von Neumann from Princeton University, third candidate for "inventor of the electronic digital computer," that the idea of a stored program and other basic processes were brought to ENIAC. Before von Neumann's arrival, the computer had to be rewired every time a program was run.

Atanasoff, Eckert, and Mauchly may have moved from electro-mechanical relays to vacuum tubes and clearly contributed the most to technology, but von Neumann developed the logical side and the "software." He suggested putting the computer's operating program (instructions) within the same memory as the data to be processed. Also, it was von Neumann who first spotted analogies of human intelligence (of the very logical variety) in the mechanisms for thinking machines.

By the late 1940s Eckert, Mauchly, and others had completed the first UNIVAC (Universal Automatic Computer) and beat out IBM in selling their product to the U.S. Census Bureau. This was the last time IBM was beaten on selling large mainframe computers. There were all kinds of legal battles over patent infringements between Atanasoff, Eckert, and Mauchly. When transistors came out, however, ENIAC and UNIVAC became obsolete. Today, most pocket calculators (containing a forty-cent chip) work faster than ENIAC and UNIVAC did.

Another computer, the Mark I, was being built by IBM at

Harvard University at the same time as the ENIAC was being developed. This was the first stirring of a giant getting ready to move.

THE EVOLUTION OF PROGRAMMING

If you opened one of the mainframe computers from the 1960s, you would see a thick mass of multicolored wires connecting the machine's circuitry. These artistic networks gave access to each of the thousands of switches inside. To imagine how this collection of switches works, you could use the analogy of a large city building. If you had fuses in every window and blew them out in a special pattern (say the shape of a star), every time you turned the lights on you would see that star pattern. That is how the early computers worked, and that is what goes on in a microchip.

To change the program of an early computer, you had to rewire the whole thing. Then, as now, a program told the computer which switches (fuses) to turn on or off. The computer read the program by finding an electronic pulse that opened or closed a certain set of switches. The main way this was done was to sense where minute spots on a reel of tape were located or where the holes in a punched card allowed current to flow through. Experiments with decimal system computers in the mid 1940s were not successful. So all computers now use only a binary code—0 (off) or 1 (on). School children call this base 2. This means that the form of the machine code is simply on-off, yes-no, or right-wrong. Figure 1-1 shows the binary code through the number 12 and the comparable decimal system number.

Each of these pieces of data was called a binary digit (bit). Sets of eight bits were arranged together to make a byte, which is usually the equivalent of a character. The large computers had as many as 16,000 bytes of memory (16K). For comparison, the computers most often used in schools have between 48,000

Binary   Decimal

  0 ---------------------------- 0

  1 ---------------------------- 1

 10 ---------------------------- 2

 11 ---------------------------- 3

100 ---------------------------- 4

101 ---------------------------- 5

110 ---------------------------- 6

111 ---------------------------- 7

1000 ---------------------------- 8

1001 ---------------------------- 9

1010 ---------------------------- 10

1011 ---------------------------- 11

1100 ---------------------------- 12

FIGURE 1-1.

(48K) and 126,000 (126K) bytes of memory. The amount of memory is expanding quickly. In fact, some of us who work in universities are already designing educational programs for IBM's "3-M machine" which will have 3 million bytes of memory for quickly carrying data, voice, and pictures throughout a vast communication net. Apple is working on a similar personal computer that should be ready in 1987.

In the 1950s programming researchers got bored with the time-consuming process of using machine language and developed higher level languages that took care of much of the tedium for them. COBOL (for business) and FORTRAN (for science) were developed at this time. These high level languages translate English-like instructions into the binary code the computer uses.

THE TRANSISTOR

In 1945, three scientists at Bell Laboratories came up with a very simple timing device called the transistor (transfer resistance). This device was simply a sandwich of semiconductors—mostly germanium. Silicon became popular later. By 1950, Bell Telephone had built the first solid-state (transistorized) computer. Built like an old radio with wires connecting each component, it was called the Leprechaun. In another ten years one of the three inventors of the transistor, William Shockley, would set up the first microchip factory in what was to become California's Silicon Valley.

FROM THE MICROCHIP
TO THE APPLE GENERATION

The microchip (which is Babbage's large engine on a postage-stamp-size silicon chip) became the central part of the microcomputer. IBM made a bad decision—to wait until the microcomputer was a "safer" area. Small companies, like Apple, jumped into the new personal computer field.

Although Steve Jobs can be given credit for selling the Apple II microcomputer, it was Stephen Wozniak who created it. If Wozniak (who is *still* working on his college degree at the University of California at Berkeley) had not built that machine, there is no telling how long it would have taken teams of experts from places like MIT, Cal Tech, and Stanford to take the microchip out of the lab and convince some company to put it into our living rooms. Working in his garage, "Woz" came up with a model that still impresses electrical engineers for its artistic, simple, and elegant design. Developing the disk controller (disk drive) was the only technological breakthrough, but the notion of one man's bringing all those diverse elements together from so many sources is truly amazing.

COMPUTERS IN THE WORKPLACE

Business is moving beyond spreadsheet analysis and word processing to data management. In other words, the computer is coming into its own as a communication device that can structure information in a more usable form, capable of growing and changing as more information is added to the system. Computers can take dictation with 95 percent accuracy, proofread, and even send off a corrected version automatically. Although we cannot afford machines that can type from speech today, we will exit the decade talking to our microcomputers.

In company after company, there is a reemphasis on production and process engineering. Computers can read bar codes on grocery store items and record the torque applied to individual screws on an assembly line product. A central computer can even reprogram manufacturing tools and robots—enabling a factory to meet changes in consumer demand. The mainframe central computer assumes control over the less-sophisticated tools (robots and the like) that supply the brute force of the factory. The newer factory computer systems can even diagnose their own ills and lead technicians step-by-step through the process of repair. Sensors play a large part in automation and give computers their ability to see, hear, sense temperature changes, and even smell. Odor sensors have been installed in some factories in which dangerous fumes are a potential hazard.

But what about the workers during our boom-and-bust economic cycles? Firms themselves can recover from economic crises, but workers often may not. Increasingly when companies need workers, they turn to robot technology or computerization of the workplace. Sometimes workers aren't able to go back to old jobs, and new workers never get the chance to come in. During the Industrial Revolution, workers often were able to move into other jobs. It was difficult then; now it will be even more difficult. When economic value is increased by knowledge rather than labor, we have a very difficult situation. And, as computers take over knowledge functions, this problem will heat up. Already we have had our first post-industrial strikes. Telephone company employees, for example, picketed the same computer installations that enabled operations to continue as usual during the strike by human workers.

Japanese workers have unionized against robots taking over their highly skilled jobs. One Japanese worker left in a fully computerized factory said in a television documentary: "Sometimes I feel that my hands could cry because their skill, acquired over so many years, has been taken away from them."

Automation has gone beyond replacing blue collar workers to replacing specialized office clerks and white collar workers. How are intellectuals and middle managers going to respond as expert systems and decision support programs take their places? Microelectronics weaken the link between employees and a firm's success. Of course, what we may have here is a wealth redistribution problem, not an automation problem. If computer-controlled robots can do work that humans should never have done, they can save humans for jobs that let the brain function at a highly creative level. Now we just have to find someone to pay for such work.

COMPUTERS IN OUR PERSONAL LIVES

It used to be fairly easy for the wrong person (and difficult for the right person) to gain access to computer personal data banks. While that is still true, to a degree, we now have state and national laws that allow only "proper" access.

Schools have a major role to play in developing computer awareness, and educators have contributed to the development of four basic safeguards:

1. creation control
2. content control

3. access control
4. technical safety control

The Freedom of Information Act and other legislation have allowed the individual more access to whatever is in his or her file. The information can then be challenged, changed, or at least a disagreement noted. Since the late 1960s, laws have steadily been passed that forbid secret data banks and protect personal information on both telephone lines and over the air. But much remains to be done to protect the public. Some states still sell information on driver's licenses, and some colleges sell information on graduates. In the future, this intentional misuse of data will, it is hoped, be forbidden.

We are moving in the direction of registering (logging) all entries into data banks and notifying the person involved. The individual can then question all entries and can sue if the wrong person gets access to his file. In addition, the penalties for casually pulling information from one file to another are becoming more severe.

Although most of the changes over the last two decades have been in the direction of more personal safeguards, we must demand more and continue to be vigilant. The cost is certainly high, but computers can be used to hurt people. Fortunately, however, they can also be used to help people. It is up to us to help decide how computers will be used. The only limit is our intelligence and creativity.

COMPUTERS IN EDUCATION

Historically, as teachers got their hands on more and more educational technology, namely books, they were freed from some of the more mundane instructional tasks. They were called upon to be more sensitive to a child's individual needs and to teach a much wider range of subjects at greater intellectual depths. Will

computers have the same result and require the already overbur-
dened, underpaid teachers to take on yet more responsibility?
Surprisingly, the answer is yes! But it is to be hoped that society
will be more sympathetic than in the past by granting more
money for schools and teacher salaries. We get the kind of
teachers we deserve. With a looming teacher shortage and
greater intellectual demand we must attract our best and bright-
est students to the field. And we will attract neither the number
nor the type we need unless teachers are viewed as well compen-
sated professionals who make independent decisions.

In spite of often not having needed materials (paper, books,
and even chalk) and in spite of inadequate facilities, there is a
certain joy in teaching. Doing something where you can make a
difference, watching individuals grow, and making a contribution toward the solution of human problems have always been
rewarding. Having a new tool—the computer—gives many
teachers the feeling of being real pioneers, and they are determined to enjoy it.

There is a major historical difference in the way microcomputers are coming into the classroom. The trend is from the bottom (students and teachers) up. This is in sharp contrast to the
usual top-down approach to educational innovations.

Nothing in educational history, other than the printed book,
has a wider range of potential applications than computers.
Students will have electronic information/knowledge devices to
use in learning throughout their lives. And, surprisingly, computers in education can actually provide the opportunity for
human interaction. While computers provide many opportunities, there are *no guarantees.*

Lessons from the Business World

American industry now recognizes that "working smarter" is
a better productivity strategy than working longer and harder.
Managers at all levels ask hard questions about computer procedures, systems, and people. If it is difficult to identify who is

doing what and why, often a computer is the answer. Businesses first look at their operations to see where a particular type of computer would fit in. They talk with everyone in their facilities and with people outside their organizations. When a current system is determined to be flawed, businesses look those facts in the eye and get on with making changes. So it must be as well with education. Although the educational market is small in comparison, school personnel would do well to ask similar questions:

1. Do we need a computer in our school?
2. What work are we going to do with a computer?
3. With what kinds of specific problems can the computer help?
4. What are the benefits and what are the costs?
5. Are there operational enhancements?
6. Is this the time to buy?

Another lesson that can be learned from the business world is the need for lifelong learning to counteract planned obsolescence. Business at every level has been quick to link up with universities and governmental agencies (the Department of Defense is a well-financed example). Perhaps the schools as well could link up with businesses and local government agencies, thus gaining access to better equipment and better preparing students for the real world.

Since our world is rapidly changing, it is important for educators to recognize that a more general, theoretical, and philosophical education (which includes the arts) may be more helpful in dealing with rapid change than on-the-job skills training.

Libraries: A Key Element in the Computer Equity Issue

As the educational role of computers increases, so also does the issue of who benefits from this powerful technology. Since minority students are most apt to be found in poorer school districts that often are unable to afford computers, the gap between the "haves" and "have nots" may continue to widen.

A related problem of sex equity also occurs. If computers are used in secondary school math classes, where most often the boys outnumber the girls, girls often come out on the short end. Also the stereotype that boys are more mechanical than girls can be a limiting factor in computer access by girls.

Today our schools are working with a much higher percentage of economically deprived students. If this generation of students ends up being less educated than the previous one, we have to look beyond the schools to socioeconomic equity. This will cause us to bring all our institutions—from business to the family—to bear on improving schooling.

Historically, libraries have played a major role in giving citizens equal access to information technology, namely books. Far from becoming obsolete, libraries could become a key element in the equalizing process. Already many libraries now check out computer programs, or even portable computers. Others keep the machines in the library and require users to bring their own programs. Whatever the combination of elements, libraries are important in keeping technological change more socioeconomically equitable. Just as they gave everyone a chance to read books, they may become an important factor in providing computer services to those who otherwise would not be able to afford a computer at home or to those in poorer school districts.

In the more wealthy school districts, which already have microcomputers, the school library can be used to bring parents into the educational process. A school library program in one of the school districts I work with has set up a program where, if a parent comes in and assumes responsibility, students can check out portable computers overnight. Not only are parents brought into the learning process, but individual students who are economically worse off are brought up to par educationally. And as soon as a cheap optical scanning device (computer peripheral) becomes available, these students will be able to view any book in the local or national library on their computer monitor. In the future computers will be a major factor in the pattern of both education and social change.

IN SUMMARY

More computers have come into schools in the last ten months than in the previous ten years. The challenge is for the teacher to learn to be a facilitator of the learning process rather than the source of knowledge. Children cannot live in a vacuum. The teacher must be an adult with something to offer and must help direct these rapid changes.

Learning is everyone's concern. Our country's social and economic well-being depends on how well we educate people for a literacy-intensive technological world. If computers can assist us in the teaching process then there is good reason to welcome their appearance.

Chapter 2

The Computer as an Agent of Change

One of my older college students recently said, "The difference today is that the future is not what it used to be." In fact, one-fourth of the jobs today did not exist in 1970. We are living through a real transformation similar to changes that occurred during the Industrial Revolution: there were shifts in all areas; nothing could stop them; hardly anyone saw them coming; and it was all over before most people knew what was happening. True innovation occurs when you cannot go back to the way it was. Computers are a true innovation, unique among technologies. The permanent changes that computers bring confront educators with a new challenge, that of preparing ourselves and our students to participate in an ongoing series of technological changes.

This chapter sets teachers out on the path of computer awareness—the first step in understanding how computers are changing our world and what they mean for all our social institutions, including education.

We must not only react to change, we must be able to make informed choices, cope comfortably with computer-related technology, and make creative applications. At least some of us will need to go on to make positive innovations. Where do we begin? First, let us look at how computers can impact both the world and the classroom and explore the potential of innovations like telecommunications, artificial intelligence, and robotics. We will examine both uses and abuses of computer technology and take a glance at what the future of computers could have in store for all of us. Whether for a brief workshop program or an indepth university course, this is the most convenient place to begin in teacher training.

THE COMPUTER AS A CATALYST
FOR REVITALIZING EDUCATION

The computer revolution is here. It is changing, for better or for worse, the way teachers do things. These new machines are also acting as a catalyst for generating new insights into the whole learning process. When you bring a computer into the classroom, things naturally change. Some changes can be anticipated; others cannot. Some changes are desirable; others are not. But, for sure, things will never be the same again. And, yes, it is possible to find ways in which machines and people interact that offer psychological comfort, aesthetic pleasure, and societal reaction.

Hopefully, the computer presence will cause us to think not just more about computers but also more about education. For instance, educators can become involved in curriculum reform by considering what should be taught by computers and what should not; why computers increase student motivation to learn; how computer-related activities can be integrated into the curriculum; how to go beyond simplistic drill and practice; how to accommodate the exponential growth of new knowledge; and, generally, how to prepare for a new "learning society" made possible by the computer presence. Simulation, video conferencing, laboratory experimentation, problem solving, writing/reading, and creative/artistic projects via the computer already are available to meet our needs. Still, the computer will not solve all our problems. More likely, it will create a whole new set of problems.

CAN A COMPUTER POSSESS
THE QUALITIES OF A GOOD TEACHER?

Desirable qualities computers offer include objectivity, knowledge, patience, and endurance. The computer does not get tired of teaching. It holds lots of information, and it allows students to proceed at their own pace. However, a computer has undesirable qualities as well, such as speed (it does some things disconcertingly fast), accuracy (sometimes it is too precise), and insensitivity (it does not respond adequately to personal needs). Some of the most important qualities of a good teacher are not possessed by a computer . . . spontaneity, warmth, and caring.

If more teachers can connect with this powerful tool and come to see the computer as a device they can control, a technologically aware social consciousness is likely to develop. The potential of computers in developing many levels of societal understanding should not be overlooked. Video cable, telephone fiber optics, and satellites all have a role to play here. Interactive graphics and video already allow people to communicate visually, on individual computer terminals, from far corners of the globe. Computer graphics, with or without videodisc technology, can give students in diverse locations the opportunity to jointly visualize phenomena that they ordinarily encounter in abstract form.

HOW COMMUNICATION LINKS
EXPAND YOUR VIEW

When computer networks provide worldwide, instantaneous communication, there is high emotional impact with real potential for reducing intergroup conflict. This is especially true when television, live graphics, or videodisc libraries are brought into the network, for they can portray the full freshness of human diversity sympathetically while highlighting common experiences and concerns. There is the potential here for a change in psychological orientation—identifying with different cultures, yet in ways that respect diversity.

Informal networks, involving a very few individuals, have always been an area of trust and a springboard for action between and within societies. Computer conferencing is simply a powerful extension, involving more people, of that concept. It is now possible to turn to a diverse structure— individual micro-computers—that would allow participants to join the dialogue, using machine translation so language is not a barrier. Communication can take place at any time from any location, and past statements are not lost as the interaction progresses. Computer conferencing may be a first step toward a revolutionary network of international interaction. The technical resources are now here—and they are being connected. The broadening of participation in a powerful dialogue may be a key to identifying ourselves with the entire interdependent species on a worldwide basis.

Technology takes on a momentum of its own—without waiting for human understanding. It certainly has broad interpretations for human survival. The same high technology that could destroy us in a nuclear war may turn out to hold the key to human survival.

ARTIFICIAL INTELLIGENCE: FROM THE LABORATORY TO OUR LIVES

In addition to teleconferencing and networking, computers have already entered our lives in surprising ways—from entertainment to information processing. Even updating our basic industries will require a reliance on large-scale integration of machine intelligence and knowledge technology. With a growing number of workers in knowledge/information occupations, whoever controls the information revolution has some form of increased control—whether personal or geopolitical. And whoever (whether corporation or nation-state) builds the next generation of computers will have an enormous technological and commercial advantage.

Just as the industrial revolution levered our muscle power, the computer revolution is in the process of levering our mental powers. We are now capable of building computers that are very nearly self-replicating and can themselves be used to build even smarter and more powerful machines. Intelligence, as we know it, has slowly evolved using DNA as its base. Now a new intelligence may be emerging—one that does not require a specialized environment providing air, water, and nutrients and one that does not have to go to school. Simply by being linked together, computers can learn from one another at the speed of light. And, just as airplanes do not fly on the same principles as birds, artificial thinking may progress into something very different from our own biologically based intelligence. As this may suggest, the leading edge of computer science has no fixed laws and is highly experimental. In fact, it is akin to a black art.

A LITTLE HEALTHY
SKEPTICISM AND CONCERN

Various technological futures have been oversold by the mass media, by technologists, and frequently by the public itself. The Western countries have had to put up with technology hype for more than a century. Sometimes cynicism creeps in.

When I took my first science class in college, I remember the professor confidently predicting that "computers were just a passing fad that would have no long-term impact." That aroused my interest, and I enrolled in a computer science class the following semester. This was in the late 1960s, and the professor who taught the course was part of a team that was working on language translation for the U.S. Air Force. He was sure that computers were the answer to everything. Millions of dollars were allocated and spent translating into English tons of articles— many from journals that the Russians had translated, without machine assistance, from English. The results were often laughable. For example, the expression "out of sight, out of mind" became "invisible idiot." And, the sentence "the spirit is strong, but the flesh is weak" became "the vodka is excellent, but the meat is rotten." Finally, the Air Force gave up and cancelled all contracts for computer translation.

Early broken promises by computer experts on everything

from translation to management information systems to office automation have been conveniently forgotten. Although these innovations were only supposed to take a few years to work out, fifteen years later we are just beginning to come up with solutions. Even with inexpensive new microcomputers, nearly half of all small businesses report that they do not quickly return the money invested in them. And, the *Wall Street Journal* concluded that computers would not be cost effective in their newsroom.

The whole issue of ethics and privacy is another concern in the use of computers. For example, IBM sold some computers to the Chilean Secret Police. And, although the computers themselves do nothing wrong, they allow that organization to go about its work more efficiently.

The power of technology can easily be misused. Information is control—and our wisdom in using this control usually lags behind our ability to concentrate information. For example, census data banks, which are supposed to be protected, have, on occasion, been tied into certain FBI data banks—according to material released under the Freedom of Information Act.

Some television cable companies gather information on the backgrounds and viewing habits of their customers. They are able to monitor which programs are being watched by electronically checking the customer's TV set. In one court case against a pornographic film, lawyers obtained a list of viewers from a local cable channel to prove that it did not violate community standards.

Ironically, a two-way cable television, using computers, has great potential for turning the home into an entertainment/educational center with almost unlimited access to information.

How can we keep our privacy from becoming entangled in the electronic web of computers? To begin with, we need to educate our citizens so that they understand how information is collected and shared between public and private agencies. The public needs to have knowledge of the capacity of the new technology and the potential dangers associated with an information society.

Is what has been called "adolescent lust" for our own technology decadent? This, in turn, leads to another question regarding our love affair with computers: What happens if our trust in computers turns out to be a dangerous mistake?

Films dating back to the 1960s dealt with machines causing war. In *Failsafe,* for example, actor Henry Fonda, President of the United States, says to the Soviet Premier, as New York and Moscow are blown up: "We're to blame ourselves; we let our machines get out of hand." A more recent film, *War Games,* deals with an adolescent who gains entry to the top secret North American Air Defense Command Computers. In real life, it is not possible to access the NORAD computer by telephone line as the students in the film managed to do. Signals are sent in our secret air waves, in code. It would take a great deal more than one teenager to break into that system. However, a group of junior high school students, using TRS-80s, did come within one step of shutting down the entire New York Bell telephone system—but they did not break into the Defense Department. Although no one has gotten into the NORAD computer, people have accidently tapped into secret government computers. Development tends to move faster than security!

Although *War Games* is fiction, there are valid concerns over trusting technology with more and more information, security systems protecting computers, and electronic mistakes. Our early warning computer system, under Cheyenne Mountain in Colorado, has given over 3,700 false alarms. However, only one of those went beyond a few minutes (seven minutes to be exact) and ordered our fighter planes into the air and our missiles ready. SAC bombers were not ordered off the ground because no one could reach the President or Secretary of Defense (who must order them up) in that period of time. Fortunately, an Air Force Colonel thought it odd that the Russians were attacking in a "period of detente." He checked. We were not under attack. It was a computer error. If our new "Star Wars" defense scheme goes into effect, computers will be making the decisions.

Some writers point to another concern—the commercialization and hype that surround computers. Ads on television are designed to make parents feel guilty if their children do not have a computer—a few go so far as to practically equate the lack of a home computer with child abuse. In spite of the media hype and exaggerated claims most parents and teachers look upon the new technology with a cautious euthusiasm. Some scientists feel that the idea of extending human intellect through a binary machine language consisting of a series of zeros and ones is exaggerated. Is it absurd to expect intelligent machines to open up worlds of speculation, possibility, and intellectual enrichment? Whether we like it or not, as part of how a new generation is growing up the machine does enter into social life and psychological development.

In the field of education we have had our failures with cold, repetitive, programmed learning machines (that early computer programs mimicked). Even now, the limits of our present microcomputers cause programmers to channel students into a narrow range of possible responses. The danger here is that they could be prevented from exploring the complexities of important concepts. Fortunately, computers have a great deal more branching potential than programmed learning machines, especially if they are not used as the only mode of instruction.

In the early 1970s I wrote a book on stimulation and suggested putting a computer terminal in every elementary school classroom. What I did not know was that the most primitive terminal rented (if you could get one from IBM) for $1,800 a month—not exactly within every elementary school budget, especially since the terminals had to be linked up to an unavailable computer which, even if a time-sharing agreement could be worked out, did not have programs for elementary school children. It wasn't until a few education programs and the low-cost, low-energy microcomputer came along in the late 1970s that school systems could consider using computers across grade levels.

By now, most everyone agrees that computers have "great

potential." But, as one bright fourth-grader in our lab school said when he found that comment along with Ds and Fs on his report card, "There is no greater burden than having great potential."

There are problems. In a pilot study at a small, rural California school, I found that there is a tendency to look to problems that are easily quantifiable. Some of the most important problems we have to deal with are not quantifiable. In addition, there is a tendency toward somewhat superficial questions and answers—and many users assume that the program knows more than it does. The important point here is that with all its power, the computer is not yet ready to contribute much to learning fields of knowledge (like moral philosophy, social theory, or literary criticism) that cannot be reduced to formal procedures.

Acknowledging all these problems and the feeling that there is often more smoke than fire coming from computer usage, the fact remains that artificial intelligence is moving on many fronts. Robotics, natural language understanding, image and speech recognition, cognitive modeling, problem solving, writing/reading, and simulation are but a few of the areas in which these machines can amplify human knowledge. Programs can simulate environments that are either too expensive, too dangerous, or too far in the future or past for students to experience directly. The strength of such programs lies in the challenge they pose for children to think for themselves and solve problems.

THE FUTURE—
A FIFTH GENERATION OF COMPUTERS

The first generation of computers was based on the technology of an electronic vacuum tube; the second, on a small vacuum tube; the third, on a transistor; the fourth, on an integrated circuit. The fifth generation will feature artificially intelligent machines that can *produce* information. Such computers actually make judgments and draw conclusions about input data.

We may soon reach the optimum circuit size. For example, even now, protein is being experimented with as a circuit—and it is at the bacteria cell level in size.

Convinced that thinking machines are the real power of the future, in 1981 the Japanese government launched a major research effort on artificial intelligence. In the United States the private sector responded, and over a dozen companies joined to form the Microelectronics and Computer-Technology Corporation (MCC) in 1982. MCC member companies include Advanced Micro Devices, Allied, Control Data, Digital Equipment, Harris, Honeywell, Martin Marietta, Mostek, Motorola, National Cash Register, National Semiconductor, RCA, and Sperry Univac. Based in Austin, Texas, and headed by Admiral Bobby Ray Inman (former head of the CIA), MCC has impressive resources, but researchers may be playing a catch-up game with their Japanese counterparts. Fifth-generation computers could influence everything from creative expression to geopolitics.

Already Japanese machine-knowledge engineers are experimenting with a book-sized reading device that uses silicon chips, each containing the contents of several books. These "expert systems" even allow you to go from written word to sound if you would rather hear than see.

In the United States, scientists at Dartmouth University have recently put the entire contents of the *Encyclopedia Britannica* on three videodiscs, each side containing 52,000 pages. Using an Apple IIe microcomputer and about $600 worth of additional equipment—a videodisc player and connecting link—you can go from page 1 to page 35,000 in three seconds. With today's first-generation microcomputer (part of the fourth generation of computers) we can use color, video, high-resolution graphics, sound, animation, and speech synthesis and still have the capacity rapidly to manipulate data. Linking today's microcomputers to telecommunications (see Chapter 8) allows us to transmit pictures or data the same way we broadcast television signals. The process is called teleprocessing and gives us the means to link computers rapidly through the air.

Some fifth generation computers will use optical light signals, rather than electronic circuits, for computation. Older silicon chips take electronic impulses as "on" and "off" signals and convert them to light. When these electrons are pushed too closely, or through thin circuitry, the microchip can be damaged. When the photons from new optical computers cross one another, or come close together, there is no problem—the data is transferred through crystals on beams of light. Signals can be absorbed from any direction, come close together, cross on the same path and run different programs simultaneously. Optical computers are also smaller than silicon-based computers, and they are good at rapid image recognition. As a consequence, they are an important component in the "Star Wars" scheme.

By looking back to biology, we may even be able to look beyond fifth generation computers. Scientists are now considering a radically different kind of computer that is based on molecular reactions of living cells rather than silicon. Bacteria have used sophisticated chemical processes to transfer information for billions of years. Their enzymes work by stereoscopically matching their molecules with other molecules, a decision-making process that occurs more than 10,000 times a second. Using this model of biological functioning, it may be possible to build a computer that is half alive and half electronics cell.

With new developments in DNA, recombination may result in networks of "biochips" which can be bred by the millions and put to work in knowledge processing. Why? Because digital computers may have a limited potential for simulating thought, and there are styles of problem solving that may not be digitally computable. Biological science mechanisms may advance "computing" as the research curves of both areas cross.

In the future we may see a different style of computing—less rigid and working more like a brain than a machine. In fact, the "mood" of such a device might affect the way scientists solve problems. Figuring out what this will look like in the future is a little like trying to see a 747 while watching the Wright brothers at Kitty Hawk.

It is important to view both present and future advances as a *means* to communication. When technology is viewed as a means rather than an end, people can use it to stretch their imaginations and increase the number of options—which in itself is a kind of freedom. Computers, like an exciting friend, can invite us to do things that may not have even crossed our minds. Computers also force us to ask some intriguing questions:

Are we a process through which another form of intelligence is itself evolving?

What roles have and will computers play in our world?

Where is that literacy-intensive technology taking us and what are our options?

What measure of control do we really have over the machines we create?

How can we use our knowledge and influence to find out about computer applications that are good for society rather than harmful and dehumanizing?

If the current generation of students is not as well educated as the last, how can the technology help us reverse that trend?

DOONESBURY   **by Garry Trudeau**

FIGURE 2-1. DOONESBURY by G. B. Trudeau. © 1982, G. B. TRUDEAU. Reprinted with permission of Universal Press Syndicate. All rights reserved.

Will our society provide schools with the means to make their contribution to shape the future?

The answers to these questions will be determined, in part, by how well we prepare this generation of students to work with the coming generations of computers.

Chapter 3

Helping Teachers Direct Technological Change

The computer should never be used as a substitute for interacting directly with the environment. Children should paint with real paint brushes, dance real dances, and collect real flowers rather than just doing these things on a computer screen. However, these in combination with the computer can result in a certain synergism that can focus and expand the imagination of the child. In this way the computer may actually expand access to the physical and social world. Computers will depersonalize education only if we fail to use them for achieving what we desire. There is nothing in the technology that prevents the classroom environment from being filled with emotions, values, patterns, real objects, concrete materials, colorful images, and a creative intellectual/physical life. It always comes back to our discipline—a thorough knowledge of the learning process itself. The characteristics of effective instruction will assist us in incorporating the new technology into the curriculum.

Computer education will make both the teacher and the school more important, and it may give us the chance to do for all what was once possible for only a few students. Computer-based instructional technology will play a large role in bringing valuable, exciting, life-long learning experiences to many people. Even as the mystique of microcomputers in the classroom fades, we are growing to respect its usefulness.

This chapter looks at why (and how) the classroom teacher is the key to making computers work in schools, at both preservice and in-service training strategies, at the potential for using computer-wise children and teaching peers as guides, as well as at suggested formats for training sessions and software evaluation. How teachers and students feel about what they are doing has a lot to do with whether a computer education program is good or bad. The chapter concludes with some points to consider when a teacher decides to bring a computer into the classroom.

—The computer has the potential to be an instrument of freedom.
—Teachers should reject the control aspects of computing and be central to the decision-making process.
—Courseware and software are only a part of the action; the rest depends on the teacher.

TEACHERS INFLUENCING THE MARKETPLACE

One of the more clever devices for facilitating teacher control of the new technology is the National Education Association (NEA) Educational Computer Service. This teacher-controlled service will assess, endorse, and even market computer software. NEA designed the service in response to the institutional needs of teachers for high-quality software.

This teacher-to-teacher service will examine and catalog public domain (nonprofit) agencies. Teachers throughout North America, commercial publishers, and the public are encouraged to submit software that they have developed for use in the classroom. The NEA Educational Computer Service will market those of highest quality. With nearly two million members, this collaborative computer service shows a great deal of promise in providing teachers with better courseware and teacher-to-teacher advice in making the most effective use of computer-based technology.

THE CLASSROOM TEACHER:
KEY TO MEANINGFUL CHANGE

The speed with which the computer has been plugged into almost every aspect of American life is unprecedented in the history of technological development. The effects may be both unanticipated and unintended. In addition to shaping change, computers may be the most important example since the printing press of a technology causing major educational change. Still, one key element—the teacher—is crucial to the success and proper implementation of any new learning tool. Yet even very enthusiastic teachers may be intimidated when it comes to putting demands on publishers for good software materials.

Companies with fairly high standards for printed material are often abandoning those standards in the commercial rush to make computer materials available. Teachers need assistance in recognizing quality materials and in attitude change. In a survey to determine the best uses of computers in California classrooms, I expected to find a number of common elements in those computer curriculum programs judged "best." I was wrong. The one common variable was the *teacher* and the teacher's attitude toward change.

More changes have been attempted in education in the past decade than in the previous century. Unfortunately, most of these efforts have not moved very far beyond the rhetorical or organizational stage. In spite of the best intentions, new ideas have rarely had much lasting effect on how children learn. Schools are conservative by nature and slow to respond to changing conditions. A number of studies indicate that the principal reason actual changes in children's learning have been slow has to do with one factor—the classroom teacher.

More specifically, some of these same studies indicate that the teacher's attitude toward learning is more important than providing new methods and program structures. Good organizational arrangements and techniques may be successful in changing the learning environment in terms of new materials, resources, and spatial relationships. But new organizational arrangements are rarely successful in changing the way the teacher views the learning situation, especially when it is the attitude of the teacher that is so critical.

The problem of changing teachers' attitudes toward learning often seems unsolvable. Even well-financed and carefully thought-out programs may have little or no effect. The Ford Foundation's Comprehensive School Improvement Program is just one example of failure to bring about significant changes. In explaining their lack of success, the CSI Program people cited *conservatism of teachers* as the major roadblock to reform. It was reported that "teachers often reacted to any form of openness, lack of structure and independent student activities as a threat to discipline." The program's evaluators reported that, even when exposed to working examples of new techniques, teachers were reluctant to pay more than lip service to the ideas generated by a successful innovation. In fact, it was reported that attempts to change teachers' attitudes often resulted in an increased resistance to new ideas.

For several years, I have been working with programs designed to change the behavior of classroom teachers. The goal has been to provide the means whereby teachers can come to accept technological innovation (namely, computers). To organize educational change around teachers requires that we build a system that encourages teachers to become expert in and enthusiastic about computers.

Usually teachers are asked to implement new techniques along lines which have been already worked out by others. Sometimes a committee of teachers is selected to take part in a kind of sandbox democracy—the purpose being to give the "appearance" of teacher participation in making curricular decisions. Whether such inconsequential groups are formed or not, classroom teachers usually have little real power in deciding what innovations they will be expected to carry out in their classes. As a result of this lack of power or real involvement in reaching decisions, teachers may feel little commitment, if not actual resistance, to the called-for innovations. Small wonder that real changes are not properly implemented in the classroom when the agents of change—classroom teachers—have no real desire to change!

If innovation and changed attitudes do not result from mandates or sandbox democratic decisions, how then can innovations reach the classroom? The literature on cognitive dissonance lends support to the notion that mandates from above are not sufficient to bring about such change and points out that self-direction is of crucial importance in attitude change. The implication is that change increases and is more permanent when the person feels that he or she has freely chosen to alter his or her point of view. An advantage to helping teachers work with computers is the fact that these tools were first brought into the classroom by *teachers*.

In addition, the same assumptions we make about children and their learning suggest possibilities for helping teachers themselves in learning new attitudes and implementing new methods. The teacher who has both the right and the competence to make important decisions will strive toward new ideals and new behavior in a positive manner when in a proper environment. In other words, personal responsibility and voluntary choice, made in a setting that assists in making that choice a reality, have positive results. An essential factor in this positive environment is that the leader or authority figure is seen as a resource person or point of reference, not one who mandates what is to be learned. The possibility suggested is that, in the proper environment— rich in human, material and experiential resources—the teacher should have the opportunity to make decisions about what new ideas to assume or put into effect in the classroom.

Furthermore, if teachers, as a group, have a hand in making the decisions and suggesting what changes are desirable, such changes will then take on greater credibility and authenticity than if the "experts" or authority figures initiate the type and direction of change. Self-influence and peer group influence increase both the likelihood and the intensity of change.

THE TEACHER AS DECISION MAKER

With most schools scheduled to put microcomputers into classroom use, teachers need both information on the hardware and a good software evaluation system. Microcomputer use in the classroom suffers more from lack of information and misinformation than any other educational technology. If teachers aren't able to set the standards for instructional courseware, no one else will. The general staff, top-down approach to selection will not be nearly as effective, and computers might go the way of educational television—one more good educational tool that didn't reach its potential.

Computer use in the classroom may be the first major change to move from the bottom of the educational hierarchy up, rather than from the top down. In attempting to encourage experimentation with new ideas and techniques, it is helpful to involve teachers in situations in which they can see results following their *own* interests in using the computer as a learning tool. Teachers need to experience various computing processes. Quite simply, the computer enables them to offer more to children.

Through these direct experiences of exploring the dimensions of what they might offer to children, teachers often change how they view their roles and come to a new understanding of what learning is all about. In the case of computers, this includes not only becoming more comfortable with the associated attitudes but also with the accompanying techniques. Thus, there often comes into being an expectation of success. This, and the teacher's perception of who he or she is and what he or she is becoming, helps to formulate goals and act upon convictions. The real test of whether change has actually occurred is the teacher's willingness to implement new ideas in the classroom.

In addition to inner supports that help individual teachers to carry through change, support from colleagues and administrators can facilitate a teacher's change process. It is particularly advantageous when teachers and administrators from the same school enroll in a workshop together and experience the process cooperatively.

TEACHER TRAINING AND STAFF DEVELOPMENT IN COMPUTERS

Confidence, trust, support, and personal experience play an important role in a teacher's ability to decide to assume a new attitude toward learning and to experiment with new ideas. Another critical ingredient to successful teaching with computers is the teacher's own frame of reference—the manner in which the teacher perceives himself or herself. Vital is the teacher's feeling that what he or she is doing is right. And, in order to have that feeling, the teacher needs both trust and confidence in his or her own ability and the children's ability to grow and change.

In the supportive, relaxed atmosphere of a workshop, teachers can be provided with opportunities to experience new computer techniques that they might choose to use with children—simulation games, writing on the computers, computer-assisted instruction, and other good open-ended activities like the building of adventure stories. They can also experiment with a wide range of materials for potential use with children. Through such experimentation with interactive activities and learning materials, teachers may experience a new perception of both their own and the child's relationship to computers.

Figure 3-1 shows the levels of computer knowledge. For many people, awareness is the only necessary level. However,

Levels of Computer Knowledge

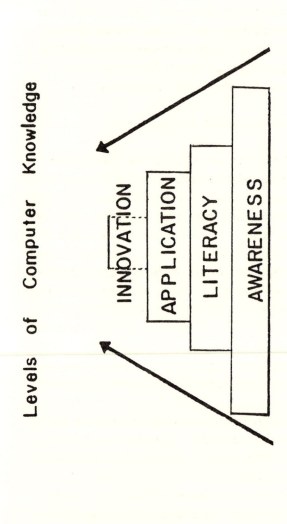

INNOVATION
APPLICATION
LITERACY
AWARENESS

Teachers should strive for the application level in order to use computers successfully in the classroom and prepare students for the future.

teachers should strive to reach the application level in order to use computers most successfully in the classrooms and prepare students for the future. With regard to the literacy level, one thing is certain: computer literacy, like virtue, means different things to different people; but it definitely means more than collecting computer languages. It means being able to cope comfortably and effectively with computer-related technology.

Some General Guidelines for Staff Development

1. All sorts of people need to be involved, not simply those with computer backgrounds. In fact, excellent facilitators may not be computer experts. It is always a good idea to develop some local "experts" for on-site, long-term training.

2. Awareness must be developed. What are the district's resources and what is happening right now? What plans are being readied to help the staff become aware of the power of the microcomputer? Decision makers at all levels must be involved. Site principals, for example, can see how record-keeping, test-generation, and word-processing programs can help them in their daily lives.

3. Teacher training needs more than nuts and bolts. The program must be based on research, theory, and good educational practice.

4. Staff development activities undertaken in isolation from day-to-day activities seldom have impact. Teachers must not only be involved, they must be able to relate professional learning to their ongoing classroom routine.

5. Teachers need to be able to evaluate software and courseware. Will the program improve the educative process? Being able to check things like reading level and whether or not the program models sound educational strategies is most important. After all, it is the classroom teacher who must integrate computer materials into the curriculum. Some suggestions: Do some things wrong (you know the children will). Where does the pro-

gram go when mistakes are made? Is there a provision for early exit? Does it allow you to change things to meet your needs? Is the student response able to change the flow of the program (branching)? How much thinking interaction is involved?

6. Teachers need to pay attention to the kinds of computer applications that students are likely to encounter in the real world as well as to their direct use in learning. In fact, computers may influence future jobs and fundamentally change the educational process.

7. Staff development projects must aim at helping everyone involved in the educative process (including school board members) to use computers as effectively as possible—without crashing in the rush to eagerly accept the future.

Teacher Anxiety

Source of uneasiness: Loss of control over the teaching/learning process—fear of being replaced.

What can be done to help: Develop a list of the instructional things that can be done better by the teacher. Discuss the complementary role of teacher and computer. Point out how the computer can actually give the teacher more power.

Source of uneasiness: Mechanical, impersonal approach to education.

What can be done to help: Stress the personalizing role when teaching other students. Working together can increase opportunities for mutual help and socialization.

Source of uneasiness: Feeling that it is too late in career to begin.

What can be done to help: Provide for small immediate steps—friendly programs.

Source of uneasiness: Using different computers that are often confusing and incompatible.

What can be done to help: Provide hands-on experience and information on efforts to make the equipment compatible. Avoid technical jargon.

Needs Assessment

Before any training effort begins, the workshop leader must have some information about the characteristics and needs of the teachers participating. All teachers will need to learn some information about technology and some computing skills, but individual needs will vary. The elementary reading specialist will have very different needs from the high school chemistry teacher. Teachers will also enter classes and workshops at different levels of computer sophistication. Some teachers will be timid beginners, in need of very basic information; others will be working at the application level, ready for exploration of new ways to use computers in their classrooms.

A needs assessment will enable the trainer to be sensitive to the participants' individual situations. The assessment itself may consist of informal chats or structured written surveys. The trainer's job is to gather needs statements and begin to prioritize them. This process should be shared with the teachers, involving them in shaping the direction of the training. If there is a wide discrepancy in the group members' needs and experiences, certain participants may take on the role of trainer at some point; peer tutoring and special projects may also be arranged. Here it may be useful to provide a specific example of how to construct a workshop.

A SUGGESTED FORMAT FOR TRAINING SESSIONS

Children as Teachers

To begin with, identify children and young adults in the community who have had experience with word processing, spreadsheet analysis, and some programming in Logo, PILOT, or BASIC. These students will act as tutors for the workshop participants. After some initial work with children, the participants teach each other (peer tutoring), and a mix of films, speakers, and field trips are added.

Workshop Materials

For a session with 15-20 participants, a staff of two leaders and a technician are needed. The leaders can alternate the presentation of new material with exercises to be carried out by the teacher trainees. While participants are working on the exercises, the workshop leader circulates around the room to give help. A technician is vital to setting up the room for each session and keeping the systems operating properly.

Every effort is made to have each participant seated in front of his or her own microcomputer with enough space to spread out papers, manuals, diskettes, and other materials.

A microverter is used so that participants will be able to tune to the output of their own system's video monitor on one TV channel and switch to what is on the workshop leader's screen by simply changing to another channel. This allows the participants to model what they will subsequently be required to do.

Topics to Be Covered

The topics to be covered in a workshop that introduces teachers to computers are shown in Figure 3-2.

In the first session participants spend a great deal of time attaining familiarity with the microcomputer itself—the keyboard, the television monitor, the printer, and the disk drives. Participants go through the mechanics of turning the system on and off, typing, correcting errors, cataloging a disk, running a saved program, initializing a blank diskette, and using peripherals (such as speech synthesizers and videodiscs) until these hardware tasks can be accomplished routinely. This is a good time to cover briefly the history of computers, future social impact, what a computer is, the functions of the central processer, long-term memory, random access memory, and the fact that the computer does its work under instructions programmed into its software.

INTRODUCING TEACHERS TO COMPUTERS

1. Define a computer (history, role in society, potential for education, ethics).

2. Set up hardware and run some instructional software.

3. Evaluate sample courseware and instructional software.

4. Develop strategies for integrating computers into participants' classrooms.

47

As far as this session is concerned, once participants understand the background information and can tell the computer how to do the things they want it to do, they are "computer literate." Whether or not this new literacy is as important as many claim, it is perceived as important. And although many of us object to the term, there are many reasons why knowing something about such an influential technology is better for an informed citizenry than being ignorant of it.

While it is true that most users of computers today do not know any programming language and that new programs that do the programming are coming onto the scene, it is also true that people who understand the rudiments of programming tend not to believe that the program knows more than it does. So many aspects of our lives are computerized that some understanding of programming is useful simply for responsible citizenship.

With authoring systems becoming available that allow users to program in standard English, that is then translated into a computer language, there is no intention to turn trainees into programmers. However, an understanding of some of the basic concepts of programming tends to make users more effective and creative in using whatever hardware and software they have available. Using programs in Logo, PILOT, and other higher-level languages like BASIC and PASCAL, teachers can change and create lessons. The main factor in the workshop is time. We have to be content with conveying the general idea of programming and giving participants a simple authoring system that transcribes their English commands into a computer language.

Use of Commercial Software

Imagine what it would have been like if someone had invented the stereo five years before they made stereo records. That is kind of what happened to computers and the programs designed to run on them. Workshops are based on the assumption that teacher-participants should begin with the software when using a computer in the classroom. A model is provided for evaluating commercial computer programs in the important areas of simulation and writing and for setting up a planned program that will give participants a more systematic, comprehensive, and descriptive history of available educational software. Participants investigate methods for looking at subject area, application, grade level, instructional model, program style, lesson design, and publisher. Special attention is given to such instructional concerns as:

1. *Program suitability.* Will the program work with your students and on your particular computer?
2. *Worth.* Is the program significant and worth trying with your students?
3. *Values.* What social values are reinforced by the program?
4. *Accuracy.* Is the information in the program correct?
5. *Goals.* Are the objectives of the program clear?
6. *Curriculum fit.* What are the program goals? Do they fit in with your objective?
7. *Effectiveness.* Does the program keep the students on task (through a sequence of skills that make sense to you)?
8. *Outcome.* Are the results desirable?

Evaluation and Selection of Software

The following outline provides specific information on the evaluation and selection of software. Always preview software before purchasing it. Most software can be made available to schools on a thirty-day or sixty-day trial basis.

I.   Compatibility with hardware to be used
    A. Brand and model
    B. Memory capacity (RAM)
    C. Peripherals necessary or desirable
    D. Extra equipment/languages required

II. Documentation
    A. Thorough and complete
    B. Preparatory and follow-up supplementary materials
    C. Program development information
    D. Copyright considerations
III. Configuration of users
    A. Single/multiple students
    B. Single/multiple computers
IV. Objectives for use
    A. Appropriate subject area and use
        1. Appropriate reading difficulty level
        2. Consistent concept level
        3. Relationship to identified curricular objectives
    B. Sound, consistent educational strategies
    C. Content
        1. Accurate
        2. Educational value
        3. Free of stereotypes (about race, ethnicity, etc.)
    D. Instructional quality
        1. Provides well-defined purpose
        2. Achieves defined purpose
        3. Presents content cleanly and logically
V. Program execution
    A. Runs smoothly—ERROR FREE
    B. Provides for exit before completion
VI. Program design
    A. Student management
        1. Record and score keeping
            a. Types of scores/information available
            b. Number of students program is able to manage
        2. Lesson assignment
            a. Easy to review and alter lesson sequence
            b. Option for assignments by computer
        3. Program branching for individualized instruction

B. Student response modes
   1. Question format
   2. Motor skills difficulty
   3. Interactive program flow
C. Color, sound, graphics (optional?)
VII. The bottom line—DO YOU LIKE IT?

In coping with software evaluation, participants are encouraged to think about these more general questions regarding educational programs:

1. Are they interactive (the strong point of computers)?
2. Is there a lot of feedback?
3. Are they able to simulate the participant when he or she is not there?
4. What do you want the computer to do and not do, and how does the program fit into this scheme?
5. Does the program allow you to individualize?
6. Will it save you time?
7. Can students create and use aspects of that creation with other members of their class?
8. Does the program wait to act on command, allowing the student time to think about the answer?
9. What kind of teaching/learning style is modeled?
10. Does it motivate children and offer them different levels of difficulty?

It is assumed that the usefulness of any computer program cannot be appraised in isolation—a program's effectiveness and quality must be judged with an implementation in mind. Do not assume that the programmer knows more about instruction than you do. One alphabet program distributed by a major publisher had the writing moving from right to left; any first-grade teacher in the country could have spotted that problem. Since the development of educational software is in its infancy, teachers need to be in decision-making roles.

SUMMARY

Implementing computers in the classroom requires more than mechanical change by the teacher. There is the extremely important element of personal change. A teacher putting the new tool to work in the classroom may experience a change that goes well beyond materials or techniques. There is the potential for change in the whole spirit of the classroom, with the teacher acting as a resource person, assisting learning in a more informal, independent, and noncoercive environment. Far from making the classroom more sterile and mechanical, the unique interactive properties of the computer can result in changes in both techniques and teacher attitude. Just about everyone working with children and schools is in favor of more individualization and student independence, and the computer allows us to move on both fronts.

Having computers in the homes may bring parents into a closer partnership with schools—a partnership generally considered essential but usually lacking. Parents often enjoy being invited into a participatory role, and availability of computers in the home may be a motivating factor for parents to become involved in their child's schoolwork. There are some problems that stand in the way of closer school/home partnerships: scarcity of computers in poorer homes, software problems, and a few parents and teachers who are unwilling or unable to become involved as educational allies.

In spite of the fact that many students have computers at home, the school classroom will be the primary place where becoming informed about the implications of computer-based technology will occur. This includes the social impact of computers, computer application, problem solving, and how computers work.

In spite of the exaggerations and continued hype, the new technology requires different skills to operate and provides us with some additional tools to teach those skills. The new information/knowledge occupations require people who can think and handle complex intellectual tasks. This, in turn, requires lifelong learning to keep skills up-to-date. The traditional school was designed for an industrial society that was built on a limited range of basic skills, routine-repetitive tasks, and a high degree of time consciousness. As we move into this new era, we must continue to search for the possible negative effects of both our classroom practice and what appears to be a positive new technology.

For the foreseeable future, classrooms of some sort will surely exist. Children need learning professionals, equipment, and the company of other children in the learning process. The computer is just another powerful tool in the process. As such, it can give everybody more control over learning and even shed some light on how we communicate and on human learning itself. Computers could even help make the classroom a very different place—a place where both teacher and student can exist as total human beings, reacting and interacting effectively with one another.

Chapter 4

Using Computers to Enhance Learning

Many of the elementary school children that we are working with today will graduate from college in the twenty-first century. Most of their lives will be spent relearning how to swim in a sea of information and images. In this literacy intensive environment computer-controlled systems will reason, draw conclusions, make judgments, and interact through multi-sensory, image-rich programs. Mixing print and imagery, computer technology will be used to access, convert, and tailor information in a manner and context that is most usable for the individual learner.

Just as it took time for movies to move beyond simply filming a play to become a unique art form, it has taken some time for computer programs to move beyond the rather boring scope of drill-and-practice and traditional workbook-like instruction. As has been pointed out, the potential exists for computer literacy, music composition, art, writing/reading, simulation, problem solving, and experimentation. The computer can be a workbook page, a language experience story, a science experiment, a four-dimensional model, a tutor, or the fantasy world of interactive children's literature. In this chapter we sample a variety of exciting ways in which computers can help teachers and students learn.

Computers are being written about and discussed as an important frontier of modern thought and education. We can learn a great deal about both by listening to the discussion as we go through the process of sorting out what skills can and should make use of computer-based technology. To move toward the fulfillment of human learning potential we, as teachers, have to examine the computer as part of our cultural landscape and learn how to use it to reach our learning objectives. A human teacher can respond sensitively to students' learning problems. We have no such guarantee with computers. In our effort to use the interactive capacities of a computer to their fullest, we must move beyond traditional instructional methods and learn to view the machines as objects to think and learn with. And, as these computer devices are developed, we can gain fresh insight into the nature of human learning itself.

DON'T FALL INTO THE SAME TRAP
AS EDUCATIONAL TELEVISION

Students who use computers primarily for repetitive drill, in place of interaction, will become very bored. One teacher reported that his students were getting tired of working with computers. Upon examination, it turned out that the only thing the students did were some rather boring Science Research Associate (SRA) cards. It is important to remember that the same mistake was made in the school use of television in the sixties and seventies. Required to watch video presentations that were poorly made and difficult to see on small classroom monitors, students came to associate those tedious lectures with any school use of television. The result was that more interactive uses of that medium of instruction were never given a chance. Teachers must demand first-rate software materials so that one more good instructional tool, the computer, doesn't get put aside.

BORROW FROM OTHER FIELDS

Business, the military, government, industry, medicine, basic research, media, and communications have all gotten more attention from hardware and software manufacturers than has education. As a result, these fields have developed better programs and more advanced ways of using computers. Educators have already borrowed word processing, spreadsheet analysis, high-resolution graphics, sound synthesizers, and simulation. As long as original intent is recognized, there is no harm in adopting computer uses from the world that we prepare our students to enter. In addition, we can change and build on these outside tools. In fact, this whole process may prove useful in preparing students for their social/ vocational roles.

COMPUTER-ASSISTED INSTRUCTION

Computer-assisted instruction (CAI) involves the use of the computer as an aid to teaching a particular subject. In the 1960s many projects were started, primarily at the secondary level, using large mainframe computers. Not only was early instruction primitive, but costs were so high that few schools could afford CAI systems. By the 1970s some CAI programs that went beyond drill, testing, and programmed learning had been developed for large time-sharing computers. Special terminals with good graphics and touch-sensitive video screens were used to communicate with the computer. However, the cost remained high, and we were into the 1980s before some of these programs were available for use with the much more attainable microcomputers. Even beyond the factors of cost and shortage of programs, many people feel that CAI never really attempted to use the full interactive potential of the computer. The major problem seemed to be the inability of the format to challenge students to explore a hypothesis of their own or speculate about the material being studied.

COMPUTER-MANAGED INSTRUCTION

Computer-managed instruction (CMI) uses the computer as a recordkeeper, overseeing instruction and directing students elsewhere for actual learning. A CMI system can assign a student to answer a set of questions, read a book, listen to a tape, or whatever. It collects and processes student information—interests, background, learning records, etc.—and can give suggestions for various ways to learn certain topics. It can also supply this information, in a summarized form, to the teacher so that he or she can help the student choose alternative steps in learning various subjects.

A typical CMI recordkeeping program begins by asking for the teacher's name and the classes that will use the instructional program. Whenever the teacher wants to use the program, he or she must type in the class in which it is being used.

Example: WHAT IS YOUR NAME
MR. MARK KIGER
THE CLASSES ARE:
1. ENGLISH 1
2. ENGLISH 2

The computer then gives the teacher a table to choose from. In most CMI programs, the teacher must use a manual to know what the abbreviations in the program stand for and fill in all the numbers for every assignment to be made.

It has to be done like this for each individual in class. It is very time consuming and a bit confusing. And, although it can be adapted as a simple electronic gradebook, we have to ask whether that part of the task can't be done as well in the traditional manner.

Like CAI, computer-managed instruction was developed for the expensive mainframe computers. It was also frequently tied to the behavioral objectives movement of the sixties. CMI was based on clearly specifying behavioral objectives and using the computer to measure a student's performance based on these objectives. After the student's work was measured, the CMI system would prescribe material to help the student reach a predetermined competency level. This "teach-test-record and prescribe" approach has been redesigned for microcomputer systems.

However, the real potential of computers lies in areas beyond both CMI and CAI.

COMPUTERS AND EXCEPTIONAL CHILDREN

Exceptional children—students who need special education programs—will use computer technology in unique ways. Many gifted children will go beyond computer literacy to create new applications and innovations. Teachers of gifted and talented students are faced with the task of teaching advanced computer-related skills and with providing a supportive classroom atmosphere in which eager and curious students may become truly innovative.

Students with physical disabilities are experiencing new sensations due to microcomputer chips that allow them to see, hear, talk, and walk. Researchers at Wright State University in Ohio used computer parts from a local electronics store in Ohio to build a complex system that can simulate the body's electrical impulses to the muscles. As a result, a young woman who had been paralyzed since an auto accident was able to ride a bicycle and take a few steps.

In our work on computer vision, we had to examine how the human brain stores information about the use and function of objects. It turns out that we separate objects by their shape and function. This permits us to recognize things whose function is impossible to describe. Our learning-disabled students often have disruptions in processing information. Working with computer visual processing brings together artificial intelligence, special education neurophysiology, psychology, and philosophy.

In the classroom, students with learning and developmental handicaps are benefiting from increasingly sophisticated instructional software. Computer-based instruction has the potential to analyze a student's errors and branch the learner to a tutorial, record his or her progress, and make an appropriate assignment for the next day. All teachers can use the computer as a valuable tool for both understanding and designing individualized instruction for their students.

Computers will be a part of every child's future. Teachers who work with exceptional children, whether in a special class or in a mainstreamed situation, need to recognize that students must know about computers. There is a very real danger that learning disabled, mildly retarded, and behaviorally disordered individuals could become the "have nots" of the computer revolution. The same specialized techniques that are used to teach reading and math must also be applied to computing as it becomes a part of our definition of literacy.

Computers, Mainstreaming, and Special Education

The microcomputer, by simply attaching peripherals (especially to the Apple and IBM microcomputers) can allow the handicapped without voices to speak and those without hands to type. Basic living skills such as answering the phone, writing letters, using the television set or radio, and operating other dials are all now possible. For nonverbal students, speech synthesizers take keyboard entries and turn them into speech.

Computers can provide the handicapped with avenues of communication through which to receive information and express thoughts. The visually impaired or blind can be taught Braille by computer. The physically impaired can be given nonverbal communication capabilities. The hearing impaired can be reached by the computer using visuals and synthetic speech enhanced by vibrations.

All children should be educated in a manner that does not inhibit their interaction with peers—this reflects both the research and the law. Computers can help individualize a child's placement in the least restrictive environment. A practical way to have mainstreamed children appear in a positive light is to teach them how to use a computer first. Then, when they go into the regular classroom, they can teach the other children.

COMPUTERS—
OR MACHINE INTELLIGENCE ITSELF—
AS A SUBJECT OF INSTRUCTION

We are so dependent on computers that to shut them down would cause general economic chaos. However, the word *computer* is a little misleading. It was chosen years ago to refer to the old "number crunchers" that could only calculate. Now they work as well with words, diagrams, and speech; and they have taken on far more tasks. Whether we call it machine intelligence or artificial intelligence or computers, this topic must be included in instructional programs so that we can learn to integrate computer technology into our lives. How computers affect our society, how they do their work, and how we use and program them are important parts of any modern curriculum.

Through several home information services, already available in North America and Europe, users can tap into large data bases via phone lines or air waves and have information transmitted right into their living room. This is done using a regular television set to display written words, speech, graphics, and moving pictures.

Students need to be aware of how computers are entering every aspect of our lives: from devices we use in our homes— coffee pot, microwave oven, wrist watch—to the schools we attend, the stores where we shop, the banks that handle our money, the offices where we work, various governmental services, law enforcement, health care, transportation, even our cable television service (which keeps track of what we watch for billing purposes). Like it or not, computers are here to stay in schools, libraries, work, art, music, sports, and entertainment. We will simply have to learn to adjust.

As a subject of instruction we need to look at how computers will be controlled in the future. Especially with the convergence of research and development curves in computing, artificial intelligence, robotics, and molecular biology.

The way we communicate with computers is already being greatly expanded. We will probably exit the 1980s talking to computers rather than using keyboards. Beyond this a system is being tested on severely handicapped people who are unable to touch or speak to the computer. It allows them to communicate by simply using their eyes. The eye movement tells the computer to open or close doors and windows, turn on or off lights, televisions, radios, etc.

Experimenters are already developing a communication system that uses an electroencephalogram—a device for measuring brainwaves—to communicate with a computer. The computer compares the user's brain waves with the patterns programmed into its memory. The brain wave computer interface works, but it will be several years before problems of accuracy and speed are worked out. When they are, computers may very well come under the brain's command. One practical result might be houses wired for brainwave control of everything from appliances to door locks.

Most computer use in the future will occur outside of science and mathematics. Therefore, new computer curriculum projects must work beyond that narrow scope and examine computers across subject areas, and not just for college-bound students. If computer instruction is to succeed, it must focus on computer-based technology for all, not just for future scientists. Certainly scientists and mathematicians have no corner on the crucial computer concerns of sound reasoning and clear thought.

To begin with, students need an appreciation of the capabilities and the limitations of artificial intelligence (computers). They need a strong background in critical thinking, communication skills, and the liberal arts, as well as math and science.

With regard to computers, it is a mistake to specialize too

soon because a narrow skill can be rapidly outdated. The best opportunities are for those with a broad background. Remember, most of those who need computer skills will be employed not directly in computer science fields but rather in word-processing and information/knowledge fields like data communications. It is predicted that by the end of this century, we will all be able to afford a small-size supercomputer with more power than today's largest computers. Students will have micro-computers in elementary schools, at work, and in their homes.

A basic goal of artificial intelligence is to build and program a machine that shows some of the same traits as human intelligence. Machines should be with us, within a decade, that are able to move, see, feel, talk, hear, and possibly think. Computer-based systems may even acquire the ability to sense our needs and respond to them. Although some of these machines will be designed to function on a totally different basis than their human makers, the form and function of computers are reminiscent of biological processes.

SIMULATION GAMES

As the space shuttle tumbled out of the sky with all the grace of a huge brick, the astronauts knew that their emergency landing was in trouble. The launch rocket had failed to function properly, and they had to abort the mission and land at Dakar in Senegal, West Africa. Having no engine power for landing, they glided in toward the shortest of the three possible landing sites for the shuttle—the one that was set aside strictly for emergency landings. As the African peninsula grew larger in front of them, they realized that they would come down short of the runway. Then they heard the voice of mission control, "You can do better than that. Let's try it again." The view out of their windshield blinked, and they were back to 10,000 feet, ready to try again.

Had this been a real emergency landing, the astronauts would have died in the crash, and the space shuttle would have been two billion dollars worth of debris. Fortunately, this was a computer simulation. The shuttle's flying characteristics, sounds, sights, and gravitational load were produced to the extent that the astronauts say the simulator flies just like the shuttle.

In addition to developing test flights for the pilots, engineers are testing new systems to see how they will hold up in a real-life situation. The space shuttle simulator also has a computer program that can mimic the flight of a new generation of jets and helicopters. Even subtle sounds, like hissing air, are accounted for by using a computer synthesizer. A three-dimensional computer graphics system is the view from each window. And the space shuttle runway, down to the last bump, is exactly like that of Dakar, the Kennedy Space Center, or Edwards Air Force Base. Visibility can change from very clear to heavy fog and from day to night. Even a little air turbulence or a flat tire can be thrown in for good measure. When there is a systems failure or mistake in pilot judgment, the pilots do not finish with a set of gory graphics. Rather, they just push a button and start again.

Computer video simulation games may now be very primitive and not very educational in those dusty arcades where children and adolescents spend time and money. However, connecting to higher computer memories, speed, graphics, and reasoning—and the essential ingredient of better software—makes for powerful educational experiences. In fact, simulations are perhaps the most exciting part of computer learning and have incredible potential.

An example that actually allows students to write part of the simulation is an adventure game called Detective. There are line constraints where the evidence disappears if the player does not reason quickly enough. Once gone, the evidence is gone for the duration of the game. In this game, simulation is combined with writing on the computer; and, at the push of a button, students can get a perfect copy from the printer.

An educational simulation uses a real-life model that allows the student to enter control data. For example, one microcomputer program allows the student to operate a nuclear power plant. The student has to produce as much energy as possible and deal with emergency situations based on real situations like the Three Mile Island disaster. This particular program even allows for increasing the "risk" factor by placing the reactor in an earthquake-prone area.

Some classroom simulations deal with chemical reactions too dangerous to allow in the classroom, and can allow students to change the mass of the earth and other planets and graphically observe the changes in our solar system. Some simulations go back in history and take part in, but may not change the direction of, historical events.

In a simulation for upper-grade elementary-school children, Oregon Trail, children are given a map on the video screen and a set of decisions to make in moving across the country. The simulation is carefully built on the actual diaries of early Oregon settlers. And, although it does not exactly replicate a particular trip, it has compiled a model of all the trips during a five-year period of time. With good graphics and accurate information on which to base their decisions, students try to make their way to Oregon. Some make it; others don't. Students may work in pairs, groups, or as individuals.

A simulation may only mimic one aspect of reality. However, the same thing could be said of many books. The teacher must be sensitive to all these factors and be able to use the computer simulation as a jumping off point for discussing the full reality.

Any simulation involves some kind of simplified representation. The simulation model may actually mimic the physical model (as with the space shuttle), involve a mental conception using print (Detective is a good example), or, like Oregon Trail, involve a combination of the two, based on a mathematical model of the relationships in the system.

Simulations are a method for representing, understanding,

and solving interdependent problems. They can help teach us much about the past, present, and future as well as everything from economic activity to physical and social behavior. The weather bureau and the United Nations are now using simulations to predict world population growth.

Inexpensive special-purpose graphics chips, when combined with other technological advances, provide very realistic moving pictures for a simulation. High-resolution moving graphics can allow you to display and create movies. You may start with a picture on the computer, but the realistic computer-generated pictures that follow could take you forward or backward in history and generate a whole scene based on one painting, pictures of the past, or an artist's conception of the future.

Researchers at MIT have developed a device that allows one to "drive" down the street of a modern city. Whichever way the "driver" turns, a realistic image of that street is generated.

With data bases becoming more accessible, simulations can be played across telephone lines, or broadcast over the air like CB radios. Various participants could be in different schools, different cities, or even in different countries.

COMPUTERS AND READING

Reading on the computer can incorporate space, time, sequence, animation, indexing, and glossary notetaking. Reading on the computer has advantages in modifiability, expandability, collapsibility, reorganization, and specification. Computers do these five things better (or at least less expensively) than books. You can be sure that the computer will not overlook things, and it can write a vocabulary list for you.

The computer can individualize how information can be cued. For example, it can capitalize important information, outline or map information from text, and even present notes that cover key issues. Patterned note taking can interact back into the text—

a central concept can be highlighted and notes relating to major issues can be drawn around it.

Given the TV monitors computers use, books may be read more quickly by good readers. Slow readers seem to do better on the computer when the print can be increased in size, speed of presentation can be altered, and graphics can be presented. It should be noted that some of these elements can increase the comprehension of good readers.

"THE COMPUTER AS PENCIL"—
READING AND WRITING
WITH MACHINE INTELLIGENCE

To use the "computer as pencil" metaphor, let's suppose there is no writing tool. Then the pencil is invented, and we propose that schools make this tool accessible to every child. Our critics would scold us with: "Do you mean the children have nothing but pencils? Is that the goal of education?" NO! It is what we can do with the tool (the computer) that counts. It is a completely new kind of learning tool that we, as teachers, now have available to us. We have been traveling down this Making Tools road for a long time (nearly two million years).

Reading and writing, flip sides of the same coin, are exciting areas in computer education. Computing is probably more like reading than any single area in the curriculum. You have decoding (a specialized vocabulary) and comprehension (a classical definition of reading). Even when students are using the computer for other subjects, they are reading.

There seems to be little disagreement over the enhancement of writing by using a word-processing program on the computer. When students write on the computer, they are highly motivated, less bothered by mistakes and corrections, and more willing to revise. They can move words, sentences, and paragraphs around until they are happy. And, since it is only done on the computer screen, mistakes don't count until they push a button and run the printer. For the first time students see their writing letter perfect, as if in a book. Schools now have software programs available that allow for more than a variety of font styles and sizes. Illustrative material from either a catalog of electronic art or from one's own design can be added. The "editor," who could be the teacher or another student, can even run a program to check spelling, grammar, illustrations, and cohesiveness. After that is done, the first printed copy can be run, bound, and put in the class library—Dewey decimal number and all. Children writing on the computer tend to experiment more, not worrying about errors and erasing until there is a hole in the paper. They compose more and develop longer stories.

Writing via the computer has had a positive influence on students' fiction, scientific reports, poems, and language stories. For language experience stories, they simply follow the philosophy of "what I can think I can say; what I can say I can write" (or "someone can write for me"); and "what is written can be read by me and others." For children who don't like to type, a peripheral device is available that allows them to print, or write in longhand, on a touch-sensitive plate; and the computer sets it up on the screen in typewriter-like print. A scribe-like style is evolving in new software programs that allows students to produce illuminated manuscripts. Recently I was helping some sixth-grade students in a classroom. One child complained, "My paper is only four pages long and my teacher says it has to be five." "Oh, that's easy," I said, "just move all the margins in—now it's five pages." You can imagine the teacher's reaction.

Another small concern involving word processing has to do with what a computer can and cannot do. One teacher reacted strongly to seeing a letter-perfect typed language experience story hot off the printer. "Look at this; the computer wrote the story for him." Well, the machine did not write the story. It did, however, give the student an exciting new pencil and sketch pad that function as an extension of the child.

Use of Computers in the Writing Process

Teachers must search for the few programs that retain the intellectual depth and wholeness of the reading and writing process. Components that should be examined include:

1. *Prewriting activities.* A clustering program on the computer can pull 100 words or phrases (rock groups, classical music, lyrics, etc.). When the children run out of ideas they can tap this data base.

2. *Writing.* There are good adaptable software programs like First Liner, Abuse, Interactive Fiction, and Eliza; and there are good word processing programs like Magic Window, Word Star, Bank Street Writer, and Scripset.

3. *Postwriting.* Here the computer can be used to check spelling and let you know how many times you use the word "and" and highlight each use.

Some children will never get handwriting down. Using a computer in the writing process will help them to see their thoughts in print for the first time.

COURSEWARE AND SOFTWARE PROBLEMS

There are problems associated with packaged programs involving long reading passages. The "reading" portion of most programs is stilted, unimaginative, and seems to have a negative influence on students who do most of their reading on the computer. Even simple questions use the lowest level of thinking. For example:

Current Version	One Alternate Version
Computer: Take a mental photograph of Dreiser's dramatic technique. Describe some important detail.	*Computer:* Imagine two people talking about Dreiser's dramatic technique. Who might these people be?

Current Version	One Alternate Version
Sherri: I don't understand what you want me to say.	
Computer: Concentrate now on seeing Dreiser's dramatic technique. What feature stands out the most. Describe. Your turn, Sherri.	*Computer:* What would _____ be saying? *Computer:* And what would _____ be saying?
Sherri: Like the setting?	
Computer: Yes, that seems okay.	
Sherri: The factory versus the hotel.	*Computer:* Suppose you were a new character suddenly introduced into the story. Where in the story would you be introduced?
Computer: That's the idea, Sherri. Give me some more information.	*Computer:* As _____, how would you feel about this situation?
Sherri: I see Hurstwood as a scab. Though he's been reduced, he still has some dignity, but the settings aren't dignified. The streets . . .	*Computer:* Describe what you and the other characters will be doing in the future.
Computer: Go on, Sherri.	
Sherri: The streets are an ugly, dismal contrast.	
Computer: Good work, Sherri.	

Much of what a person writes contains features of what he or she has read. Many problems in writing relate to poor reading (on and off the computer). Both are basic language processes that influence one another in perceptible and imperceptible ways. On a personal level, you can occasionally identify specific reading that has influenced the vocabulary, thinking, and the linguistic structure of what you write.

I asked adult student teachers in a summer workshop to bring in the book that had the most influence on their thinking and writing style, and ended up with everything from *A Guide to Bartending* (not serious) to *Bear Bryant's Approach to Football Coaching* (very serious). I was able to trace back certain of my own present-day writing inclinations to a book I read in third grade, *Paddle to the Sea.* The story involved a geographical adventure through Canada, the Great Lakes, the east coast of North America, and finally across the Atlantic to France. After reading that book, my thinking-writing process (for better or for worse) was never quite the same. Although the book was not particularly "good" literature, my own writing started to include references to maps and charts that went beyond geographical vocabulary, as well as to reflect complex language patterns and interest in diverse cultures. My knowledge of the world had been indelibly altered, and my horizons had risen from a small village community to include different regions, cultures, and countries. A whole new dimension had been opened up in a way that has influenced me to this day, through two overseas Fulbright grants to writing about diverse geographical locations.

Many authors acknowledge the influence of others on their own ideas and sentence structure. About once a year the *New York Times* asks a dozen or so major American novelists to list the recently published books that they have read. Some cite the impact of these books on their own imagination and work. This seems perfectly appropriate since good art, and science, is often an original synthesis of what has already been thought out. Some writers are quite concerned about this. One, Norman Mailer, seems to fear some kind of intangible influence on his own writing. Consequently, he says that he doesn't read any contemporary writing but his own. However, even he admits to being influenced by a preceding generation of novelists.

Writers for the *New York Times, Associated Press,* the *New York Review of Books*—in fact, for almost any journal—tend to follow very specific linguistic features found in what they have previously read in those newspapers, wire services, or journals. This is not the result of the editing process. Many writers actually study the linguistic features of a target publication and structure their writing accordingly. Some writers go through a similar process at a less conscious level. Much of how we learn to write is implicit, and it would be difficult to identify the sources. Yet, what we have read previously does exert a powerful hold over our writing.

Children's writing tends to follow the specific format of the material they are asked to read. An informal survey of some California school districts that used computers extensively indicated that children spent a great deal of their total reading time reading from the computer screen. Therefore, teachers must demand good hardware (to minimize eye strain) and better software reading material.

Present computing systems permit us to ask only certain kinds of questions and accept only certain kinds of data. This effectively closes many doors. When the only tool you have is a hammer, everything starts to look like a nail.

The linear, factual style of the text that appears on the computer screen in some programs often follows tedious patterns. And, when the students begin writing, these patterns seem to serve as a model for how to do everything from punctuation to writing one sentence per line. In a pilot study on the subject, I found strong trends indicating that the features of the models that children read were reflected in their writing. Another important finding was that children who used process-oriented programs that they could control ("The Story Machine" by Spinnaker, for example) created more elaborate linguistic structures and tended to write more complex stories. Having graphics and sound come in as they were writing on the computer also helped invigorate expression. And when students electronically share their stories (sometimes over great distances), writing on the computer becomes a form of publishing.

Combining work on the computer with good literature is a key here. Since children internalize specific linguistic features of their reading, it is important to recognize that children who read the least elaborate text will write with the least elaborate structures. Those who read the more elaborate text will write with more elaborate structures.

LANGUAGE ARTS AND THE MOST POWERFUL LEARNING TECHNOLOGY EVER DEVISED

Computer language arts need the same attention as computer math because the language arts have been dramatically altered by this new electronic medium. We need to be able to deal with the emergence of a new literature, a new form of written expression, and new dimensions in listening and speaking. As we communicate with our computer, through speech and pictures rather than more complex keyboard commands, we find that our new equipment can print out a wide range of type fonts and even add and print illustrations.

With dictionary programs and word processers that can be programmed to correct grammar, teachers of writing are now in the position of math teachers in the early 1970s when calculators became inexpensive. When is it preferable to let the computer correct mechanical errors and let the students concentrate on the writing process?

Being overexposed to computers too early can change a child's relationship to other people. Until now technology has not really touched children in their early years. Even television does not reach a two-year-old in a serious way. Yet it is already technically possible to make a computer-based machine that can interact with a child from the day he is born. But what happens when parents think these new computer programs are wonderful because they give them so much more free time?

SUGGESTIONS FOR THE TEACHER

1. Trust the child to learn—and the teacher to teach.

2. Active involvement in a language community is the best way to learn a language. It has little to do with exercises or school routines. There is a difference between rituals and literacy.

3. It is a mistake to assume that much of what children learn about language is learned in school (which may teach the more trivial aspects of language). Language is much more than vocabulary and grammar. Children won't pay attention to nonsense—they ignore what they don't understand. Children don't learn when there is no expectation of learning. Struggling to memorize results in loss of meaning. Drill on the computer can destroy language.

4. It is the job of the publishing company to sell you programs. It is the job of the teacher to know enough about learning to make instructional judgments regarding these programs. Don't be afraid. Don't be ignorant. Reject the control. Don't let publishers impose programs on you.

5. Ask these questions regarding programs: What is its use—and what does it do for the child? Does it take people out of the process; if it does, you don't have education. Does it control you (the computer has the potential for becoming the greatest control device ever invented) or do you control it?

COMPUTER-BASED LEARNING AND CHILDREN'S LITERATURE: LINKING THE TECHNOLOGICAL AND LITERARY WORLDS

Two of the more disconcerting problems facing teachers today are how to approach the new computer-based learning technology (the "new literacy") and how to overcome student indifference or sheer rejection of literature and reading (the "old literacy"). Far from being opposed to one another, we now have the ability to reach toward a fusion of the two— man's richest intellectual invention (the computer) and his most powerful medium for the use of language over time (literature). With computers, we can make the affective impact of literature immediate. People hear and see things and react to them in a different manner than when print is used alone. The result can promote an individual's understanding, interest in, and desire to read.

Computers not only change the technology of book production but the literary community's perception of language and knowledge. The new technology can be used to support reading and literature in the real world environment which is becoming increasingly literacy intensive. This implies teaching reading and literature as interdependent skills, with separations viewed as detrimental and artificial. Computer-based technology offers us new dimensions for intellectual and emotional involvement in the search for transcendent ideas through literature. It is possible for students to have intimate contact with literary concepts and intellectual model building.

Computers are central to the new set of tools that we, as teachers, have available to us to revitalize literature for children and young adults. What children read, either in a book or on a video monitor, is formative in their lives. Computers present us with the tools for enhancing and going beyond print to a new domain in literary concepts. It is the technology that gives us the potential for fundamental innovation in our approach to learning about literature. Fresh insights result from individuals playing with computer/video/print tools and techniques.

Whether using the computer or the traditional print medium (books), the goal of the children's literature and reading teacher is the same—to provide students with a variety of literary and expository material for many purposes, one of which is that such experiences can be a source of meaningful knowledge and enjoyment. The imaginative, printed expression of human experience and possibility is a literary experience when the reader interacts with it—whether that interaction is limited to the printed word or to a computer simulation. A good computer-based lesson (simulation or whatever) changes as the students react to it. This goes well beyond the old, rather deadening computer-assisted literature instruction. In fact, such a programmed learning style may very well have harmed the reputation of computers by casting them in the wrong role.

Computer-based technology can now tap vast electronic encyclopedias of literature, art, music, philosophy, history, and so on. Computers open up new ways for the student to browse and get instantly in touch with literature.

We are now reaching a new developmental stage in which access to a broad base of literature is made possible by computer-based telecommunications. Microcomputers of the type we use in schools today can tap into massive data banks containing both the text and the graphics of every children's book in large national libraries. In fact, one computer firm has been commissioned to study the feasibility of storing all recorded human knowledge in one gigantic data base. Less ambitious literary data bases are already on line for our use. Computer humanists at Oxford University have written software that allows students to get feedback on their own writing from a computerized archive of English literature. The French have thousands of literary texts dating from the seventeenth century on computer disks. A computerized treasury of French classics, along with a computerized French/English dictionary, is available to any school with a hard-disk drive and a microcomputer. The same set of classics can be purchased on a set of floppy diskettes. Other literary software materials are available that allow the student to ask the computer about the influence of one writer on another and other literary puzzles.

Creative imagination, working closely with applied technology, can open up new ways to read and interact. And it is through interaction with new computer-based media that many of our students will pick up literary concepts, particularly those children who refuse to connect with the traditional printed text.

A NEW KIND OF LITERARY FUSION: INHABITING AN AUTHOR'S ENVIRONMENT

The student interacting with literature on a computer does not have to confine himself to carefully designed (but frozen) structures of words on a page and the linear flow of events typical of books. The student could even get into the middle of the action by becoming a character in the story. As a character, he follows whatever strategy he can devise, thereby moving back and forth between creating and reading. The learner defines and redefines the structure of the story in his individual style, breaking free of the linear style of traditional print media.

The massive memory of new computers allows a new dimension in the presentation of children's literature. Putting the elements of a book into a computer memory system allows the learner to take part in the process of the interchange of ideas and set the direction and flow of events. This enables the student to gather knowledge and attain perception by a kind of dialogue. The computer memory, operating much like the human memory, is associative rather than linear. This technology reaches into other learning modes, much as a poet who, moving through thought patterns in image and sound, uncovers new metaphorical and symbolic relationships. Computers let us bring together literary information from different sources.

Literary programs available today have a great deal of action and puzzle solving but are far removed from joy-stick controlled interactive games. They rely on the printed word to cue the player's response but make little use of high-quality computer-generated graphics. An example of this sort of game is "Deadline'' from Infocom Software company. This interactive story advances something like this:

Computer: You are standing at the front door of the suspect's house.

Player: *(Responding by typing in instructions)* Enter house.

Computer: You hear footsteps inside the house. A young woman, overly thin and haggard, opens the door and greets you. "Hello," she says. "I don't know why you've come around here again. I really can't help you."

Player: Tell me about your husband again.

Computer: "He's a wonderful man and has never been involved with bad characters." A man steps out from behind the door. "Stop bothering her," he says.

Like the development of a play which depends on the actors' way of handling their roles, the development of the story depends on the players' continued participation: the plot unfolds according to his responses.

Another type of story relies less on action and more on the implications of character. Synapse Software has developed games that depend on character recognition in a particular passage of literature. For example, a panhandler might pester the student until some type of appropriate action is taken. And the story changes direction based on the student's reaction to situations in the narrative. Learning the rules of the interactive story, limited though many are at present, can now be designed to help the student gain a sense of mastering certain rules of literature.

Many of our schools now have interactive simulation of stories that the students are reading. Just about every teacher that has turned on a computer has used "Lemonade Stand" or "Oregon Trail." There is general agreement that these computer-generated lessons can help increase reading comprehension.

A more adventurous computer program called "Human Edge" allows a student to probe the mind of either a character in the story or the author, using a few known characteristics. This type of advanced program requires a primitive level of reasoning and a number of quick, logical inferences by the computer. To take part in this literature activity, the student only needs language skills in English. However, the programmer uses the computer language Prolog (rather than Logo, BASIC, or Pascal) because it is designed for logical inferences. Soon we will be able to program in realistic video images like those used in aircraft simulators used by NASA and the airline industry. Upcoming adventures in literature will be surprisingly lifelike.

The computer may allow us to go back beyond the mechanical Industrial Revolution (with its uniform and rigid medium of printed books) to individually tailored manuscripts and the magic of spoken language that preceded it. Although printed books are a marvelous medium for the presentation of ideas and will continue to be, a new technology is arising that allows us to interact associatively—orally, artistically, and experientially—with literary ideas. This intellectual process contrasts sharply with decoding the sequence of ideas fixed on the printed page. This new technology will never totally replace the old: rhetoric continued after the development of script writing and script writing continued after the printed book.

There is nothing inherently wrong with these new possibilities for electronic interaction with literary ideas. Some of the possibilities are surprising. For example, after reading several research studies that indicated that calligraphy improved handwriting, we used an Apple IIe computer and a #75 Koala pad to design and to print documents that looked like medieval manuscripts. Using this type of peripheral device, the children saw the similarity between drawing and writing. The individually unique pages were then carefully bound and placed in the class library. In recognition of the twentieth century, we even put a Dewey decimal number on the back. Since we could use the computer to print out multiple copies, students were encouraged to make notes in the margins as they read, much like the owners of medieval manuscripts. However, we also stored the program on a floppy disk so that other children could add graphics and change the structure at will. Using a speech synthesizer, realistic graphics, and an authoring system so that the children could program in plain English, they built simulations so that others could share their work. As we got closer and closer to conversing with computers in plain English, we made the technology more accessible to a wider range of people.

MULTIPLE-IDEA ARRANGEMENTS FOR TECHNOLOGY AND LITERATURE: COMBINING LEARNING TOOLS

A number of new combinations of books, computers, and television programs are cropping up, producing a kind of synergism. One example is a new television series designed by the Bank Street College of Education and sponsored by the U.S. Office of Education—"The Voyage of the Mimi." It is broadcast nationally on PBS and fuses standard television and book formats onto interactive computer simulations. The action seen on television is connected to computer activities distributed to school districts on microcomputer diskettes. Books are also supplied so that teachers and students may integrate the three media. The U.S. military has also built training programs that combine the strengths of each of these learning modes. While none of these media alone may be electrifying, together they provide us with wonderful opportunities to teach literature.

Learning can increase dramatically in a setting where microcomputers simulate what scientists do, where television brings in actual moving pictures of the experience, and print materials are combined in the process to reinforce the learning experience. Each of these possibilities can be downloaded directly from telecommunication networks to school microcomputers, videotape, and printers (so that the printed material can be put into a folder or bound for student use).

BRIDGING THE GAP BETWEEN
TECHNOLOGY AND LITERATURE:
TELECOMMUNICATION NETWORKS
AVAILABLE TODAY

Chatting. Chatting back and forth to communicate is simply using a computer much like a telephone except that communication is usually in print on a television monitor. Like the telephone, you need another person at the other end. Machines that can translate and speak in a human manner are not yet a reality. Scientists are, however, working to understand the linguistic principles that would enable such machines to be built.

Electronic mail. As the name implies, this is like regular mail, except that the letter moves at the speed of light to the addressee's computer.

Electronic bulletin boards. These are like electronic mail, but public. Anyone with a modem-equipped microcomputer, and in some cases an access code, can view them.

Conferences. Individual groups in diverse locations can instantly communicate questions and answers back and forth. Conferencing is particularly effective with the new computer-based video devices that allow participants to see one another on a split screen. New, inexpensive digital compressors, attached to a microcomputer, allow color television pictures to be transmitted, computer to computer, on regular telephone lines.

Documents. Students in different locations write a story together or jointly interact with a literary concept.

Library. This contains both documents and software. Students can upload or download software or documents from them. Smart publishers are starting to use such libraries as distribution outlets. These libraries are also starting to include expert systems, a computer program containing the elements of an expert's decision-making behavior. In this manner, libraries will allow microcomputer users to interact with notable writers and literary experts. Computer programs now exist to allow the computer to read printed text to students, which is especially useful for the very young. The computer can read the text looking for specific concepts and stop to read out loud particular passages.

The elements that make up these possibilities are in place in many schools today. However, human technological advance is so rapid that we often fail to assimilate intelligently the possibilities that we create. Technological developments in computing, video, and telecommunications have the potential of dramatically transforming educational activities.

INFLUENCING THE NEW MEDIUM: WINDOWS ON THE LITERARY WORLD

Although the utility of computer-based learning is with us today, it would be a mistake to judge the future role of the computer in children's literature by what is available now. In the machine, literary directions are being opened up as programmers constantly develop new approaches. This situation is similar to the development of printing in its initial stages. The first printed works were poor, handcrafted imitations of manuscripts. It was only later that mass productions of literary texts started rolling off the assembly lines with standard print styles. This type of book more than halved the time required to read the text. The new technology changed the literary community's perception of language, reading, and the acquisition of knowledge.

Schools and libraries must play a role in this latest technological change or they will leave the direction of change to the teenage entertainment marketplace as parents bring such computer material directly into the home. If we abdicate our responsibilities, a promising technological art may end up like most commercial television today, taking our children's time without giving anything substantive in return. The deadening possibilities of new technologies may be glimpsed in the popular phenomenon of video games. Why not take the technologies available and use them to serve our own ends, having children and young adults enter into and learn to grow with literary traditions?

At the moment, narrowly trained programmers are making many of the decisions for us. Without the involvement of our best literary and educational minds, we could lose much in the rush from print to an electronic learning medium. It would be wise to remember the fifteenth century, when editors (the programmers of that era), in their eagerness to get out a printed book, would buy a manuscript and keep only what they thought would sell, without consulting anyone, as they set their type. The rest was discarded and lost forever.

Computers impinge on some fundamental questions of education. This new learning tool is not neutral—tools never are. They create a culture that can use and operate them. Computers are not good or bad. They are powerful. The educational possibilities for using this computer-based knowledge for human interaction, stimulation, and experience are endless. With authors like Arthur C. Clarke, Ray Bradbury, and Robert Heinlein already involved in creating software, there is a certain technological momentum. It seems appropriate that science fiction writers are creating the first interactive fiction for children and many adults. We already have some interactive fiction on the microcomputer software market; even in its primitive state, it is engrossing numerous players. Players think of new ways to eliminate evil in enchanted lands or change the characters and settings of Huck Finn, for example. The projection of the student's self into stories and situations can be as exciting and challenging as turning the page on a conventional, printed story. In putting the new computer-based technology to literary purposes, literature, like current music and art, will have to stop insisting on a purely linear perspective. We cannot slow the momentum of technological development, nor would we want to, but we can still affect the direction of the blast.

THE FUTURE OF OUR CHILDREN'S
LITERACY DEPENDS ON YOU

For the last several hundred years, the printed book has been the repository of our literary heritage as well as the primary means of understanding, preserving, and disseminating the collective wisdom of mankind. The book has been a critical part of how the child and young adult interacts with the environment. Printed books will not be replaced. But just as printed books challenged manuscripts in the fifteenth century, books are being challenged today by computers and electronic devices, and computer data bases are challenging libraries.

Electronic literature can be collected, reorganized, molded, and transmitted in order to teach to a student's particular learning style. And the first tools for the creative interaction of students, computers, and literature have already been fashioned. We must take care to preserve the unique concept of the printed book while at the same time making literature more accessible by use of the modern interactive possibilities of computer-based learning. The result can be the synthesis of literature and the computer (including video). The combination is capable of accomplishing learning tasks that neither of them can do alone. The combination will have greater range than either alone and potentially will be more human. Technology can bring energy to the process of learning. And literature can bring intellectual depth and understanding to the enterprise.

This electronic literature allows access in all kinds of unique ways. As new concepts in electronic literature come into being, it is important to avoid simply moving toward the lowest common denominator, like the crassness of most of our television and video games. The future of our children's literacy depends on what the literary community and educators do today.

The new generation of symbolic processing machines supports a large knowledge base, allows for very fast association retrieval, and makes logical inferences. We will soon be talking to these machines, showing them pictures, and becoming active characters in the stories that have been transcribed onto electronic computer disks.

Four hundred years ago, manuscripts were torn up and thrown away in the printer's haste to set everything in type. Much of what failed to make the conversion was lost. Many ancient Greek authors never reached us, and all of the manuscripts in Byzantium that were never printed were destroyed. Some of the best of a thousand-year tradition of literature was lost as the new medium turned out the popular as quickly as possible. The future of our children's literacy depends on how we put these new mind machines to work for us.

EXAGGERATED CLAIMS

Experience should make us wary of dramatic positive *or* negative claims. Edison was clearly wrong when he wrote that the phonograph would revolutionize public education. And the U.S. Patent Office was equally wrong when it suggested closing in 1890 because everything of use had been invented. Exaggerated claims in either direction can kill any new instructional tool before it has a chance to reach its potential.

The Overly Negative

Computers are simply symbol manipulators, inherently unable to understand or teach anything—John Searle

The tawdry power of video games gives us a glimpse of the future power and madness of computers. These machines will alienate children from both literature and the real world. If computers replace the book in the classroom, we will turn our children into psychopaths, because psychopaths do everything effortlessly, freely, without any sense of inhibition or suppression—Robert J. Sardello

The *Teachers' College Record* recently had a bout of computer/teacher bashing. They reported that new teaching methods never reach into the classroom because of the conservatism of teachers. In the same breath, they claim educators are prone to jump on any bandwagon. Computing is "uncritical fadism—it has no soul!"

> Word processing can spoil writers—and the creation of new literature—because it is more simplistic and sloppy (in style) than when writing implied a certain permanence . . . the medium overwhelms the message.

The Overly Positive

> Computers can do a much better job of teaching reading and literature than either teachers or schools. In fact, in our plan for a model city in Minnesota, there are no schools or libraries. Students learn at home (by computer)—Don Glines

Richard Cyert, President of Carnegie-Mellon University, says that computer programs are now available that give students sophisticated information more efficiently than books. Computers allow students to deal with and simulate real world problems of great intellectual depth. And they can graphically illustrate concepts that were in the past dealt with by imagination or mathematical equation. Cyert maintains that "This whole process will allow students to actually read less and still cut at least one year off a four year degree program."

UPI reports on conclusions drawn from an Illinois education project: "To function in a computer dominated environment, every student must be imprinted with the most important of all literacies—computer literacy (including programming in BASIC). . . . Tanya, a sixth grader who is failing all her subjects despite her sophisticated sense of style and her passionate interest in language, learns to write almost immediately upon being introduced to a computer. It turns out that she simply found her childish handwriting too shameful.''

TEN GENERALIZATIONS ABOUT EDUCATIONAL COMPUTING SUPPORTED BY RESEARCH

1. A variety of students can and do learn from the use of computers to aid instruction.
2. Teachers will remain the key to good instruction—computers will not replace them.
3. Time frames for learning are either slowed or quickened with computer instruction.
4. Computers can be misused (or underused) in educational settings.
5. Student motivation for learning may be improved with computers. The holding power of these machines must not be underestimated.
6. Management of anxiety and other human problems are major factors for teachers and students new to computers.
7. Interactive computer learning (with peers) seems far more effective than drill and practice on the computer alone.
8. Teachers and administrators need to be computer literate to integrate computers into the classroom and make them effective.
9. The teaching/learning potential for instructional computing is increasing as the technology develops. (The technology is changing so rapidly that studies are often dated before they come out.)
10. It is extremely difficult to measure the effectiveness of computer-assisted instruction empirically over a broad spectrum of experiences or subject areas. (The concepts here are based on a literature synthesis by Howard Zimmerman, California State University.)

The educational benefits of technology are still in dispute. Many studies that show student gains in classes using computers can be explained by the novelty of the machines and the effort that went into teaching the computerized courses. Technology is often viewed as the vehicle that delivers instruction. And it's the quality of the goods, rather than the truck, that most influences student achievement.

Chapter 5

Programming

The raw material for the silicon chips that make microcomputers work is sand. If I have no program to tell my microcomputer what to do, I might as well save myself a lot of money and just bring a bag of sand into my classroom. It would be just about as functional as my programless computer, maybe more so.

Programming, or telling the computer what to do, does have a role in the curriculum. Teachers and students need to have at least some knowledge of what programming is. Although computer literacy is more than simply collecting languages, knowing something about programming takes the mystery out of computers and the way they work.

This chapter on programming explores its role in the classroom and considers the most common higher-level languages used in education: Logo, PILOT, and BASIC. You are encouraged to experiment with some simple BASIC commands.

COMPUTER PROGRAMMING:
READING/WRITING RELATIONSHIPS

Reading skills are improved by simple programming activities. To program, students must perceive relationships (an important part of both reading and writing). For example, parts of a program are often not right next to each other, but they are related. Students need to know the vocabulary to spot those relationships so that, when a program is carried out, they know what to do.

Even a very simple set of programming skills, like those contained in Logo, requires the young child to make use of language in developing clear descriptions, decoding symbols, developing vocabulary, making inferences, gaining an understanding of sequencing, and using comprehensive skills (important concerns in learning to read and write). The research on children's programming in Logo suggests that they become articulate, self-aware, and confident learners—a plus for all curriculum areas and students. It does seem, however, that students at both ends of the spectrum profit most.

In programming, children must learn a variety of skills. For example:

Mastering rules of syntax. The rules in computer programming languages are essentially like the rules of syntax in general. There is an order, a structure, that must be consistently followed if the program is to be read by the computer. The following examples illustrate proper and improper syntax in BASIC:

a. LET A + B = X   [incorrect]
b. LET X = A + B   [correct]
c. IF A = Y AND X THEN PRINT
   "GREAT!"   [correct]

Mastering a sight vocabulary. The BASIC language has a number of words that are referred to as reserved words. Each reserved word must be used in a very specific way. In other words, each word has a specific function in a BASIC program statement. For the young programmer, the following list will provide adequate programming power:

a. PRINT, LET, GOTO
b. READ-DATA, IF-THEN, FOR-NEXT
c. INPUT, END, REM

Enhancing visual discrimination. Skill in visual discrimination is essential in the reading act. The errors caused by the lack of this skill are readily apparent in most low-achieving readers.

In computer programming, visual discrimination is crucial. The following are examples of this need:

a. PRINT TAB (15) HERE   [incorrect]
b. PRINT TAB (15) "HERE"   [correct]

Learning to respond to semantic cues. Perhaps the most important skill is to be able to respond properly to the semantic cues in a computer program. These cues have to do with anticipated meaning, i.e., that a given cue means that a certain word or structure is going to occur later in the program. The following examples can show this:

a. If READ is used, then DATA must also be used. In a literal sense, the computer will either look for DATA if READ is encountered, or will ignore DATA if READ is not encountered.
b. If FOR is used, a NEXT must follow, appropriately, further down the program. The computer must find NEXT if it encounters FOR.

Comprehension. Skills strengthened in noting exact detail, grasping the sequence of events, following a set of directions, interpreting the organization, perceiving relationships, anticipating outcomes, and identifying antecedent events result in the development of reading comprehension.

Figures 5-1 and 5-2 show the reading skills used in programming and a programming sequence.

WHERE DOES PROGRAMMING FIT INTO THE CURRICULUM?

Some kind of computer programming courses have been offered at the high school and college level for years. They were usually taught by math departments that seemed more intent on

Reading Skills Used in Programming

■ Mastery of a sight vocabulary

■ Use of explicit rules and syntax

■ Comprehension of whole program

■ Response to semantic cues

■ Proofreading of program

FIGURE 5-1.

PROGRAMMING SEQUENCE

010 IDENTIFY THE PROBLEM TO BE SOLVED

020 PLAN POSSIBLE SOLUTIONS (FLOWCHARTS)

030 CODE THE SOLUTION IN PROGRAMMING
LANGUAGE

040 RUN THE PROGRAM ON A COMPUTER

050 REVISE THE PROGRAM AS NEEDED

FIGURE 5-2.

93

teaching students advanced calculus than about computer courses. In my first computer course, the professor spent a month teaching us physics. I finally realized that the only physics I needed to run a computer was to understand the basic electrical principle of "on" and "off."

With microcomputers now reaching across the curriculum areas down into the elementary school level and with the dramatic increase in computer use throughout society, we must reexamine the importance of learning to program computers. The first reaction, in the early eighties, was to extend the teaching of computer programming to all grades. It was felt that this was important for citizenship and general intellectual abilities. Unfortunately, unlike the foreign languages they resemble, various computer languages were shifting in importance in unpredictable ways. There was always the danger of tying up a great deal of time in teaching a language (BASIC, for example) only to find that the field was moving on to another (possibly PASCAL).

Most people who use computers (in word processing, for example) never need to program. Still, the most commonly heard argument for teaching programming is the notion that we are preparing students for computer-related careers. However, the speed with which industry and business are changing can make these prevocational programming courses rapidly obsolete.

Vocational forecasters are still telling us about the 80-percent increase in need for programmers over the next three years. What they don't tell us is what is going to happen in four or five years. Ironically, the advancement of computer technology will cause many of these new programmers to be unemployed.

While expert systems enhance the work of professionals such as geologists and physicians, they too may decrease the number of human experts that are needed. Many middle-level computer jobs (repairing both software and hardware) are being replaced by the computer. Knowledge systems now exist for medical diagnosis, manufacturing, chemical analysis, genetic engineering, and equipment failure diagnosis. Computers have been designed with the ability to spot and repair program and mechanical problems within their own systems. As the knowledge base, problem-solving ability, and human-machine interface expands, these machines can even design programs for themselves. This leads to another concern regarding the teaching of programming. Programs that program for us and new equipment that deals with a human user in normal conversational language are difficult to accept for those of us who have spent many a tedious year learning the various programming languages. We don't want to see our hard-earned skills become obsolete.

Our best argument, then, for teaching programming is not to prepare students for computer-related careers but rather to assist in the development of social and intellectual functioning. Perhaps the most convenient argument today for teaching programming, across grade levels, is that some understanding of how programs work gives students a more realistic understanding of what programs can do and helps them function effectively in a society increasingly dependent on the information/knowledge technology.

Another convincing argument for teaching programming has to do with learning logical thinking/reasoning skills that may prove useful in other subject areas.

HIGHER-LEVEL LANGUAGES

In the early days of computing, the computer's binary code was used in programming. We call this type of communication *machine language*— the actual language of the computer. When we use higher-level languages like BASIC and PILOT, the computer translates our instructions into machine language, which uses a series of ones and zeros. It would require a machine language code similar to the following to instruct the computer simply to add two numbers together:

10100101	00100000
01100101	00100001
10000101	00100010

As you can see, a complex task would be difficult, time consuming, and tedious to program in machine language. So we use shortcuts, or higher-level languages. Some languages are better for solving problems than others. So hundreds of languages were developed. However, only a half dozen or so came into common usage. The most common higher-level languages used in education are Logo, PILOT, and BASIC. Fortunately, most computers are able to "speak" some version of more than one language.

INFALLIBLE PROGRAMS?

In my research with both children and college students I found, among students not familiar with programming, a tendency to assume that the program knew more than it did. Programs (like Eliza) through which the computer assumes the role of psychologist are taken far too seriously by students not familiar with how a computer program works.

There is a growing use of computers in reaching decisions about employment, career choice, hospitalization, incarceration, psychological assessment (and treatment), and special education placement. Although most of these reports are based on probability and need to be interpreted in an individualized manner, the computer can give them an aura of infallibility for people untrained in programming. A mythology of accuracy tends to develop (among nonprogrammers) that is simply not justified.

The lack of regulation, pirating of software, and honest purchasing of some of the psychological products on the market has put interpretive programs in the hands of computer amateurs. To interpret a computerized psychological test properly, you need to be both familiar with the limitations of programming and well trained in the discipline (psychological assessment and treatment). Some programs measure the fantasies, dreams, hopes, perceptions, and memory of an individual as that person chooses to reveal them at a particular point in time. These computer programs do not have the hard validity of scientific or medical tests—yet the uninitiated fall into the trap of pretending otherwise because the results are printed by a computer.

In the final analysis, the specific programming language taught to students may not be as important as giving programmers insight into how a computer program actually works. There are at least two other useful (nonprogramming) skills that students may pick up from learning programming language. One is the ability to control the computer, rather than vice versa. The other (as previously mentioned) relates to the thinking and reasoning skills needed to participate intelligently in an information-oriented society.

LOGO

Programs are simply sets of instructions that tell the computer what to do, how to make decisions, and prior actions.

Logo allows young children to get the computer to do some complicated things in a way that they understand and enjoy. It helps put thinking and communications skills on the same level as machine skill.

Rather than creating a long sequence of instructions in logical order, as in most computer languages, programming in Logo involves inventing new things to teach the computer and telling it what to do.

Turtle geometry is one part of Logo. Here, the child controls a make-believe robot turtle on the television screen. The child can draw pictures using words like *forward, back, left,* and *right.* Children can create geometric designs and cartoon drawings that can be seen as they work.

The turtle shows up as a small triangle on the computer screen. It responds to a child's simple commands—either typed at the keyboard; or, if the computer is equipped with a speech recognition device, the spoken word: FORWARD 50, BACK 23, RIGHT 180, LEFT 90, and so forth. FORWARD 50 moves the turtle forward 50 turtle steps, drawing a line on the screen in the process. LEFT 90 makes the turtle rotate 90 degrees to its own left.

To draw a square with the computer the child simply turns the turtle 90° at each corner of the square and makes all four sides the same length. After the child has drawn a square, he or she may want the computer to remember how to do it. This can be done by typing each direction again, while in the program mode, and then giving the program a name. The command TO followed by any name puts the computer in the program mode in most versions of Logo. With the Krell version of Logo for the Apple II, you can type the following directions using SQUARE as the name for the program:

TO SQUARE

FORWARD 100

RIGHT 90

FORWARD 100

RIGHT 90

FORWARD 100

RIGHT 90

FORWARD 100

```
RIGHT 90
END
```

Some children even figure out this shortcut:

```
TO SQUARE
REPEAT 4 [FORWARD 100 RIGHT 90]
END
```

Now, when the child types the command SQUARE, the computer carries out the new command. In this case the computer draws a square. SQUARE is now a word in the student's own computer language and it is a command the computer understands. And, it didn't have to be called SQUARE. It could have been called "Gert," "Fred," or "Dog," and the computer would still "understand" it. SQUARE can now be used with other commands to draw other, more elaborate designs like the one shown in Figure 5-3.

Logo can be used by children to create programs the first time they use a computer. And it can be used by skilled adult computer programmers in areas ranging from adventure games to scientific applications.

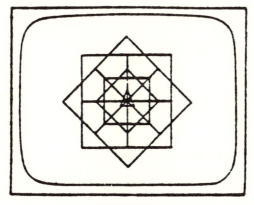

FIGURE 5-3.

Being able to "boss the computer around" (rather than vice versa) is a simple but crucial concept in the field of educational computing, and is perhaps the most important feature of Logo. The opportunity for intellectual, affective, and even social growth (when students work together) is inherent in Logo programming.

You can use Logo for geometric design, printing words, or (with some versions) singing. With Krell Logo for an Apple II, all you need to do is enter the Logo instruction SING, followed by an input to indicate a note (represented by the numbers 1 through 7) or a line. Here, for example is a sample program:

```
TO BOBBYSOX

SING 3

SING 2

SING 1

SING 2

SING 3

SING 3

END
```

The program

```
TO CHANT BOBBYSOX

BOBBYSOX

CHANT BOBBYSOX

END
```

will make the tune run endlessly. You can easily speed it up, slow it down, or change the key. Now, when you give the computer the command BOBBYSOX, the computer will "sing" the tune.

Logo can also be used for creating microworlds—small exploratory learning environments where children can develop powerful ideas through a set of self-defined interactive activities. The Logo turtle is the best known exploratory microworld. However, other Logo-based environments are equally interacting. In teacher created word-action microworlds the child can type a word on the keyboard and produce an action on the video monitor. Sprites can be used to create objects that take on a variety of shapes and move across the screen. A farm microworld, for example, might be filled with farm animals and equipment. When a child types COW, TRACTOR, or SUN into the computer the object appears on the screen. Action words like UP, DOWN, FLY, DRIVE (or whatever) set the object in motion. Typing RED, BLUE, or ORANGE changes the color. The process allows the child, through a few simple actions, to set this self-constructed world into action.

PILOT

Like Logo, BASIC, and standard English, PILOT can be spoken in many dialects. Different dialects in computer languages use slightly different procedures to do the same thing. And, unlike English, computers will run only if the right dialect is used. Fortunately, PILOT dialects are basically the same, and it usually takes only a short time to go from Apple PILOT to Atari PILOT.

Each computer has a slightly different software program that allows you to write in PILOT. In most versions the command is a single letter followed by a colon. The main PILOT instructions are a good example:

T: *Type a message.* This tells the computer to type the message that follows, usually on a television screen, not on a printer.

A: *Accept an answer.* This tells the computer to be ready to take in new information, usually the answer to a question. You must tell the computer the name of the item about which it is going to get new information.

M: *Match the key words.* The computer will compare a key word with the words or letters that you put in at the last A: statement (accept an answer).

J: *Jump to labeled line.* This tells the computer to go somewhere else in the program. The label will tell it where to go.

U: *Use a procedure.* This is like a subroutine—a short segment of the program which may be used over and over again.

R: *Remarks from the programmer.* This will allow you to make comments at certain places in the program. It will be very useful when you have to fix or change a program.

C: *Compute a result.* This tells the computer that you want it to carry out the next calculation. You must make certain that the computer has a value stored in it for everything it must use in the calculation.

E: *End a procedure.* This tells the computer to stop the subroutine and go back to the main program. Or, it tells the computer that it has reached the end of the program and should stop.

The eight main PILOT instructions shown above make up the real heart and soul of the PILOT language. These eight instructions are quite consistent among different versions of PILOT. Each version of PILOT, however, has other instructions that are used to enhance the eight main instructions. These minor or supplemental instructions vary widely from one version to another. Because versions of PILOT are so different, I will not go into further detail on this language. If you are interested in working with PILOT, you will need to work through the user's manual for whichever version you will be using.

BASIC

There are even more dialects of BASIC than there are of PILOT. So, the suggestions given here should be checked against your computer handbook for slight variations. By using BASIC, you can get the computer to do all kinds of "tricks"— print, move graphics, provide sound— just about anything a microcomputer can do. As with other languages, BASIC involves getting things into and out of the computer, comparing, doing one thing or another, deciding if something is true or false, and doing something until conditions are met.

The creation of the microprocessor by Intel Corporation enabled Apple and other companies to develop the microcomputer. This, in turn, opened new markets for software companies. Likewise, the development of computer language opened new possibilities for programmers. The rapid-fire pace of technological change in computers and communications has produced a ripple effect. When we program in a higher level language like BASIC, we can ignore what happens in the central processing unit. (It adds, subtracts, moves, stores, and compares numbers, words, symbols, and pictures.) Most educational software is written in some version of BASIC. BASIC is also more widely used than languages like PASCAL and FORTRAN because it uses more English-like words as commands.

BASIC statements are usually verbs (e.g., INPUT and PRINT) that make sense to both the programmer and the computer. These statements are always set into program lines that are numbered—usually 10, 20, 30, 40. Numbers such as 11, 12, 13, and so on, are initially reserved so that later you can insert additional statements that may occur to you. A statement is somewhat similar to a sentence written in English. It is composed of words, numbers, and symbols arranged according to certain rules. Just as key words make up statements, statements make up programs.

BASIC Commands

BASIC commands tell the computer what to do and are acted upon immediately by the computer. They give specific information about the program to the computer system.

NEW, for example, tells the computer to get ready for a new program by erasing any program statements that are currently in the computer's memory.

SAVE (plus file-name) tells the computer to save the program in memory. If you are using a disk drive, the program is saved (or stored) on the floppy diskette. If you are using a cassette, it is saved there.

LIST will produce a listing on the screen of the BASIC statements that make up the program in memory.

If you type LIST 40, the computer will display line 40.

If you type LIST 40, 60, the computer will show lines 40, 60, and all the lines in between.

RUN tells the computer to run the BASIC statements in numerical sequence.

Variables

Variables can be students' test scores, names, responses to questions, etc. Most BASIC programs include values that may vary as the program is RUN. A variable may be named (represented) by any letter of the alphabet or any letter or number up to 9: R2, D4, Z7, etc. (The Apple II computer will allow variables to have longer names that are more descriptive of what they represent.) A dollar sign, $, is added to the name of a string variable.

Only numbers can be assigned to numeric variables. For example, A can be set to equal 4, but it cannot equal JOE or BOB. The computer deals with numeric variables by treating them as values. If you assign the value 4 to the variable A, the computer treats A as having the arithmetic value of 4. Now A can be added to 2 for a total of 6, or it can be divided into 24 for an answer of 6. Nearly any character on your computer keyboard, including numbers, letters, or punctuation marks, can be assigned to string variables. For example A$ could represent 4, BOB, ?, TI4*, or anything else, but it cannot represent or equal a value. The key difference is this: string variables are not treated as *values;* numeric variables are. String variables are treated as "literals"— 4 is simply treated as the alphanumeric character 4, not as the value 4. If you assign 4 to the string variable A$ and tell the computer to add A$ to 2, you will get an error message. What the computer is saying is: I can't add characters and values. It would be the same as telling the computer to add the word BOB to the number 2, or to add a ? to the number 2. It can't be done.

It is easy to see the difference between these two types of variables if you are in front of a computer that is ready to be programmed in BASIC. Try this:

Note that in Apple II BASIC, as in most versions, any character that is assigned to a string variable must be inside quotation marks.

    10 LET A = 4

    20 LET A$ = "4"

    30 LET B$ = "BOB"

    40 PRINT AA+2

    50 PRINT A$

    60 PRINT B$

When you run this program you should see 6, 4, BOB appear on the screen. Now try adding one more program line.

    70 PRINT AA=A$+s

When you run the program with line 70 in it, you get an error message. On the Apple II computer the message says "TYPE

MISMATCH ERROR IN 70.'' Remember, in this little program, A is treated as the value 4, whereas A$ is treated as the alphanumeric character and cannot be used in any arithmetic operations.

BASIC Statements

To the *key words* (words like INPUT, PRINT, etc.) you add *statements*. If you put all these statements (which may be thought of as sentences) together, you have yourself a program (which may be thought of as a paragraph).

INPUT lets you enter (or INPUT) numeric and/or string information into a BASIC program during its execution. The information can be entered through the keyboard and is assigned to a specific variable by the program author. The variable will have the assigned value until changed by another INPUT or LET statement for that variable.

Examples: INPUT N (for numeric information)

INPUT N$ (string information is part of the statement)

PRINT causes the information to be displayed at the computer terminal. This information may be either numbers or text but must be enclosed in quotation marks in the PRINT statement.

For example: PRINT "HELLO. WHAT'S YOUR NAME?"

Result on terminal: HELLO. WHAT'S YOUR NAME?

LET is optional in most BASIC programs. It can be used to assign values to variables. The key word LET, followed by additional information, is an assignment statement. The expression may be a variable, a constant, or an arithmetic formula. Figure 5-4 shows the types of expressions.

Statement	Expression	Type
10 LET X=0	0	Numeric constant
20 LET X$="NAME"	"NAME"	Character string constant
30 LET A=4*C	4*C	Arithmetic formula
40 LET X=B	B	Numeric variable
50 LET D$=H$	H$	String variable

FIGURE 5-4.

END simply ends any program. (It isn't required on some computers.)

REM (for "remark") statements, sometimes called "documentation," are simply used to remind the programmer of what is going on. The key word REM is used to get the remark into the listing of the program. The computer skips right over REM statements when executing the program. The only way to see REM statements is to type the LIST command.

BASIC commands (Apple's version) are shown in Figure 5-5.

Although these programs may look a little difficult on paper—and at first glance—they aren't if you spend some time actually working on the computer. Logo, PILOT, and BASIC are the three programming languages that are most useful with children and young adults. And, unlike the more passive computer-assisted instruction and computer-managed instruction, you can see that the students have to think for themselves and formulate problems on their own.

Some very simplified "language type" software is now available that makes specific types of programs very easy to construct. With these authoring systems getting closer and closer to everyday speech, the problems of putting human knowledge into

SOME COMMANDS IN BASIC (APPLE'S VERSION)

NEW	computer gets ready for a new program, memory is erased
END	signals end of program
LIST	program statements in memory are displayed on screen
RUN	program is executed
SAVE	program is recorded on disk or tape
LOAD	saved program is loaded into memory
PRINT	text within quotes will show on screen as program runs
LET	assigns name or value to a memory space, defines variables
INPUT	makes place for person using program to type in data, e.g., name of student, yes/no, any number
IF-THEN	sets conditions and what to do if they are met
GOTO	directs computer to skip to certain line in program, can make loops
FOR-NEXT	makes computer perform an action a specific number of times
REM	remark for anyone reading program statements, does not affect how program runs.

FIGURE 5-5.

machine form will disappear. Perhaps the years my classmates and I spent learning the "languages" of the slide rule could serve as a caution against overemphasizing programming. In using the slide rule as a tool, some of us fell into the trap of being subdued by the technology. We spent years figuring out how to go down a path that was too difficult for anyone but a few "experts" to follow—toward a very specialized type of knowledge. Some of us even came to overrely on it and, in the process, lost the ability to figure things out on our own.

Finally, with the advent of the hand-held calculator, the slide rule and its "language" became obsolete. However, the reasoning and problem-solving skills developed in learning to use it did not. The education process itself proved useful for the future: the tedious specific skill training did not.

LEARNING ACTIVITIES

To work in the era of the technologically sophisticated workplace, we must deal with an increasingly ambiguous world. Learning to improve higher-level thinking skills and becoming more capable of seeing relationships that others may miss is not only for a small group of the highly talented. Why not provide students with good models (teachers) who believe that learning may be pursued for its own sake, as well as for specific goals?

One technique that seems to work for teachers who like to engage students is to give students parts of diverse pictures and ask them to infer relationships. With a few elements learners can discover and creatively extrapolate relationships and meaning. Figure 5-6 provides an example.

A good way to increase reading comprehension is to have

How are the following items related or not

related?
                                MEMORY

0	1	2	3
4	5	6	7
8	9	10	11
12	13	14	15

INPUT   OUTPUT

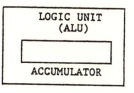

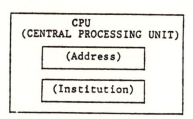

FIGURE 5-6.

students flowchart the concepts in the literature that they are reading. This will not only help with their reading comprehension, it will help in dealing with this important computer concept.

To help students understand programming terms, you can use the traditional approach of having a computer "word for the day" posted—in this case a computer programming term. Word ladders can be constructed with these words and hung from the ceiling.

Programming Shapes (the Apple Version of BASIC)

You can take your name or the name of a friend and use it to create the shape of a letter. Let's say your name is Joan. You can take that word and create a large J.

Use the space bar (the long bar at the bottom of the keyboard) to make spaces. You might want to sketch the shape first, using a ruler to make a grid over the initial so that you are sure to put in the right number of spaces. (At number 10 in the program it takes 13 spaces from the first space to the J of JOAN.)

```
Type: NEW
            10 PRINT "            JOAN"
            20 PRINT "            JOAN"
            30 PRINT "            JOAN"
            40 PRINT "            JOAN"
            50 PRINT "            JOAN"
            60 PRINT "            JOAN"
            70 PRINT "            JOAN"
            80 PRINT "            JOAN"
            90 PRINT "JOAN        JOAN"
```

```
100 PRINT "JOAN          JOAN"

110 PRINT "  JOAN        JOAN"

120 PRINT "    JOANJOANJOAN"

130 PRINT "      JOANJOAN"

140 PRINT "        JOAN"

150 END
```

Now type: RUN
and press RETURN. By putting an END at the bottom of
the program, it will stop when the program is over.

Type: LIST
and press RETURN. LIST tells the computer to list the
program in its memory. Your program will come back.
Now try replacing the 150 END command with a new
command to make a loop—just list a new 150 command.

Type: 150 GOTO 10
and press RETURN
Now type: RUN
and press RETURN and your new program will run. The
J will repeat itself over and over, in a loop. You can stop
it by pressing CTRL C.

Now try creating your own shapes and poems on the computer. (You could start every line with "I wish . . ." or simply
write lines in the shape of the described object.)

You should know that there are "bugs" (mistakes) in some
commercial diskettes and in some programs that you can copy
from computer magazines. The word *bug* came into computer
usage when one of the early large computers broke down. After
hours of work to get it "up and working," finally a moth was
found at a key junction in the computer. The term *debugging* has
been used ever since.

Try the two programs shown in Figures 5-7 and 5-8. Although they are designed for the Apple, you can use your computer manual to adjust them for an IBM, Commodore, or Atari.

PARABOLA

```
1   REM PROGRAM 5.12 (PARABOLA)
2   REM DRAWS A PARABOLA; PARAMETRIC EQUATIONS
10  CX = 140:CY = 96:SC = 1.16:FL = 0
20  P = 10
40   HGR2 : HCOLOR= 3
50   FOR T = -5 TO 5 STEP .5
60  X = 2 * P * T:Y = P * T * T
80  SX = SC * X + CX:SY = CY - Y
90   IF SX < 0 OR SX > 279 OR SY < 0 OR SY > 191
     THEN FL = 0: GOTO 120
100  IF FL = 0 THEN HPLOT SX,SY:FL = 1
110  HPLOT TO SX,SY
120  NEXT T
```

FIGURE 5-7

ROTATED PARABOLA

```
1   REM PROGRAM 5.13 (ROTATED PARABOLA)
2   REM DRAWS A TRANSLATED, ROTATED PARABOLA
10  CX = 140:CY = 96:SC = 1.16:FL = 0
20  P = 10
30  H = 10:K = -80:TH = .3:S1 = SIN (TH):C1 = COS
    (TH)
40   HGR2 : HCOLOR= 3
50   FOR T = -5 TO 5 STEP .5
60  X = 2 * P * T:Y = P * T * T
70  X1 = X * C1 - Y * S1 + H:Y1 = X * S1 + Y * C1
    + K
80  SX = SC * X1 + CX:SY = CY - Y1
90   IF SX < 0 OR SX > 279 OR SY < 0 OR SY > 191
     THEN FL = 0: GOTO 120
100  IF FL = 0 THEN HPLOT SX,SY:FL = 1
110  HPLOT TO SX,SY
120  NEXT T
```

FIGURE 5-8

Chapter 6

Don't Buy Hardware—Buy a Solution!

Sometimes the arrival of a computer in the classroom is a well-planned event. Sometimes the arrival can take the form of the proverbial baby left on the doorstep, and the teacher is expected to love and care for the computer in spite of its untimely delivery and possible limitations. Many parent organizations with good intentions and computer companies anxious to promote their product have presented teachers with computers that do not fit the needs of their students.

This chapter is designed to help you select the computer hardware (the machine itself) that will work best in your classroom. No attempt is made to tell you what brand of computer to buy. Instead, you will find help with questions to ask and important points to consider. Suggestions will also be given for introducing the wonderful new machine to your students.

MAKING DECISIONS ABOUT HARDWARE

First, decide what you want a computer to do. Second, find the program (software) you want to run. Finally, pick the equipment (hardware).

1. Start by asking everyone involved in the selection and use of the computer to draw up a list of what they want to do with the computer. Ask them to be specific. Try to reach a decision on goals.

2. Figure out what program everyone would like to run on a computer.

3. Decide on the factors (whether or not you need color, for instance) that are most important. Set your priorities; some things will be more important than others.

4. Get first-hand experience with each microcomputer that you are considering.

5. After you know your goals, have chosen your program, have set your priorities, and have had hands-on experience, you are finally ready to choose your equipment.

Things may get old quickly in computing, but we have to start somewhere. It is stimulating to be a pioneer—it can also mean, at the very beginning, you may have to take care of more of the mechanical problems yourself. Already the microcomputer has reached a stage where you don't have to worry about what is going on inside. Since future computers will be so different, it may be helpful to have several contemporary models to work with.

Technology can dramatically change the learning process. Sometimes teachers and their students exchange roles when working with computers. Although teachers are the professionals with backgrounds in learning theory, children may have an easier time getting started with computers. For example, in computer networking around the country, it is often difficult to tell whether the communication is coming from an adult or child. One adult I know received a communication that he thought was very authoritative; he later found it was from a ten-year-old.

While supervising some student teachers in California, I came upon a small group of computer-wise children and a principal who had just taken a new computer out of the box. It was plugged in and turned on—with the top panel *off.* Before anyone could stop him, the principal plugged in the language card and "blew out the brains of the computer" (the CPU). A first-grader summed it up for the children: "Boy, that's dumb!"

There are hundreds of brands of microcomputers, but the development of educational software has been concentrated on five: Apple, IBM, Commodore, TRS-80, and Atari.

Be sure that the model you buy will run your software. To run many educational programs, you must get a model that has at least 48K of memory. Some educational programs now require 64 or 128K. Many schools have built up libraries of these programs, and they will be around for some time to come. At the same time, new relatively inexpensive microcomputers are being developed by Apple, IBM, and others that have 512K of memory available for educational programs. Old machines will still have their uses. You can simply give them a single function such as word processing or programming.

THE COMPUTER'S SYSTEM

There are many ways to "talk" to a computer and for it to "talk" to you. Either *input* or *output* can be any combination of the five senses, punched cards, or even a simple on/off switch.

The *input* device can be a keyboard, an optical scanner (as in the supermarket), touch-sensitive plate, light pen (which can be moved about the TV screen to create images), and speech input/output devices. Any of these can serve as an interaction-generating instrument for collaborative learning; there is no need for solitary confinement in using the computer as a tool for individualization. Large and small group discussions are activities that can never be replaced, and the computer can be part of the process.

The *output* is how the computer "talks" to you: voice synthesizer, TV screen, monitor, printer, or (in the old days) punched cards.

The computer's *memory* is a device that stores information—either temporarily or permanently. The computer can read the information stored in its memory. The internal memory is usually made up of silicon chips within the body of the computer. External memory usually is a magnetic tape or disk on which information is stored and can be called up.

The *logic* (or arithmetic) unit is an area of the computer where logical processes (such as comparing numbers) take place.

The *central processing unit* (CPU) is the control "brain" that links everything together and carries out instructions.

THE FIRST TIME YOUR CLASS MEETS
THE COMPUTER

The following is a step-by-step approach for introducing your computer to the classroom.

1. Before you even start working with the children on a computer, it is a good idea to set it up in your home and make the silly mistakes in private. Remember, the computer is safer in your house, with homeowner's insurance, than in an uninsured school. It is important to check with your insurance carrier because a few companies exclude computers from coverage. Besides, the computer is difficult to break. And you will want to run it a lot in the beginning, during the warranty period, to see if there are problems with the system.

2. When you want to start with the children, you might begin with a small group after school, during the lunch hour, or whenever the whole class is not there. This way you develop some specialized tutors and can relax once the rest of the class gets started. This method has also been helpful with mainstreaming. By simply teaching the "special education" students first, those students, in turn, can work with the other students after your whole class introduction. This not only allows regular students to see the special students in a successful situation, but it is an excellent method for boosting their self-esteem.

3. Before the demonstration, load and use a tape or diskette so that you are familiar with it. Pick one that is fun and easy to use.

4. It is a good idea to assign some higher-level, open-minded questions as homework and/or quickly insert them at various stages of the demonstration process. For example, you can mention the idea that examining the new computer technologies today is a little like having had the opportunity (if we were alive in 1880) to look at what we might want to do about the assembly line as that concept was just getting started. Other questions can be inserted at any stage of the process: Do we want the new computer-based technologies to make work more lonely and tedious?

How are we going to ensure that workers are at least consulted about how computer-controlled equipment is designed, installed, and used? How might these technologies affect not only workers but the way the country develops and functions?

5. At least 15 minutes in advance of class (at recess or lunch), set up the computer and load the program. Run the program to be sure it works. Restart the program so that it will be ready for your students.

6. Now you are ready for the students. Be sure to seat them so that they can all see the screen.

7. Introduce your brand of computer. Young children like to say "Hello, Apple!" or whatever is appropriate.

8. If the students have had no prior introduction, show them the different parts of the computer: the keyboard, television screen (monitor), tape recorder or disk drive, and printer (if you have one). If you have a speech synthesizer (or digitizer), demonstrate how it works. Young children are almost mesmerized by a silicon accent (robotic speech). In fact, if it sounds too human, they don't pay attention as long.

9. Let two students have a go at the program while you continue your discussion. Let them know that you will schedule turns for everyone. We learn best by using our minds and our hands. The student as worker (rather than recipient) and discoverer is a good model for learning about computers. As part of the process, we need to help students exercise their minds in new and useful ways. Because of differences in social development and the very nature of computer science, girls are more likely than boys to avoid computers. Teaming boys and girls, under careful supervision, seems to help them learn to share equally.

10. Explain what a computer can do (briefly, depending on level and interest). This can be done another time since it does not require a computer. For example:

—It can add numbers very fast (e.g., in one second it can add as many numbers as a class of students could add in a whole school day).

—It can compare numbers and do something as a result. This ability makes the computer appear "smart" or even to "think."

—It can store huge amounts of information and get it back very quickly: a tape or floppy disk can store all the words in a 60-page book; some large computers can store all the words in all the books in a library in their memory and find any page in less than one second.

—It can follow directions written for it in a computer language—usually Logo, PILOT, or BASIC, when children are using it.

11. Get the class to agree to some rules for using the computer.

12. Teach students how to use the program you have chosen. Here is a sample; actual instructions will vary depending on the program:

"What is the computer asking?" (your name)

Select a student to type in his or her name.

"Nothing is happening. Why not?"

(If students don't already know, have someone come and press RETURN or ENTER.

Calling on different students, go through a sample problem and response.

Review, "What do you press to tell the computer that you are done?" (Press RETURN or ENTER.)

13. Review some of the computer rules or operations; then assign students to use the computer. Take the rest of the class off for an interesting activity. Or, if you have a small group, let them stay and watch as groups of two or four students take their turns.

14. After students get the basics, simply give them the software and ask them to teach one another.

Computer Lab versus Mainstreaming

There is nothing automatically wrong with a centralized computer lab where students gain specialized knowledge. However, individual computers should be placed in the regular classroom like any other learning tool. If you already have some learning centers, it will be easy. Just let the computer take over a center and use it in the same manner. If you don't have centers in your room, just set the computer up in a corner of the room and let small groups use it while the rest of the class is working on another task. Rotate just as you might between reading groups (the children moving rather than the equipment).

In the past, computing and programming have placed a premium on logical-mathematical ability and a narrow range of language skills. We have now reached a stage where the thinking and learning styles of both the machines and their users are more diverse. Some of the more neglected intellectual capacities are coming into play, and we are increasingly able to match computerized instructional materials and learning modes to the individual student. More of a student's mind will be cultivated, with new aspects of cognition taking a more equal status with the constricted range of thinking skills traditionally found in schools. These intelligences include musical, spatial (drawing, art, etc.), linguistic, bodily-kinesthetic (movement, dance, etc.), and intra- and interpersonal skills. The ideal of freedom is not just minimizing external constraints—it means creating optimal conditions for everyone's fullest personal development. There is no freedom in a vacuum. Schools cannot ignore the ongoing computer revolution with its accompanying transformation of the economy, communications, and social relationships. Any serious consideration of education must encompass the educating being done, and capable of being done, by the new media of communication and learning.

Chapter 7

Computer Awareness Activities

Computer literacy means much more than knowing some programming commands. It also means knowing when to use computers and when not to, how computers can improve our lives, and how their use can sometimes threaten us. In short, the computer itself is an important topic for study. The following activities for children may be adapted for many grade levels and can be worked into existing language arts, social studies, math, science, and reading curricula. These specific techniques are starting points for you and your students to explore the impact of computers in the past, present, and future.

The following activities can be used with or without computers and are useful across grade levels for discovering the structure of computerization in our society. They are designed to integrate different ability levels and help you avoid too much "teacher talk" (which is a real problem at some upper grade levels). All of the activities have proven useful for initiating highly charged student-led discussions in pairs, small groups, and whole class situations.

1. *A scrapbook on computers.* Simply have children make an illustrated book containing everything they can find about computers cut from newspapers, magazines, and advertisements put out by computer companies. This can be extended into looking for computers in current events to even a classroom art project of designing book jackets or constructing bulletin boards.

2. *Computer writing and book activity.* Use your best techniques for encouraging writing to generate stories and poems that reveal how the children feel about computers. (One story starter that I have found useful is the question: What makes a person, animal, or machine seem intelligent?)

Have your students write a scene for a film or television program they have seen about robotics or computers. Have them develop the theme of whether or not these machines are good for people or society. This can be extended to include discussions about all the ways computers enter our lives—from supermarket checkout stands, to gas stations, to instant bank tellers.

3. *Role-play newspaper reporter.* Interview people in the school and/or community to get the pros and cons about computers. Work out some good questions beforehand and try to find at least one person or business that has not had success with computers. Include these interviews in a class newspaper or put a list of what you have learned on the bulletin board. Have students look for different angles in stories on the same subject.

Gather information on computers for a class newspaper from the evening news, movies, and educational television programs. Pull out references to computers in everything from MTV to Dan Rather.

4. *A time line.* Prepare a bulletin board that represents, in pictorial form, the history of computers. Use pictures of both physical objects and personalities involved in the computer movement. You can even include some science fiction conceptualizations that the students have worked out for the future.

Looking for underlying patterns in history and human behavior might even help us understand the past and manage the present and the future. Students will better be able to complete the integration of humanity and technology if they understand the relationship between the technology of an age and its conception of man's place in the world.

As far as technology is concerned, history tells us that anticipating the effects of technological development is always difficult. How many planners, for example, foresaw that the automobile would lead to the growth of the suburbs and the decline of many inner cities?

5. *A computer dictionary.* As a vocabulary building activity, have the students put a computer-related word into a personal

and/or class dictionary. Put a picture next to the word for easy recognition. Discuss words like "bug" in computer usage. Extend this into a discussion of how any word comes into a dictionary. Have students make up a few of their own words.

6. *Creative drama—robotics and programming.* Divide the class into pairs. One person plays the programmer; the other, the robot that has to do exactly what it is told—on command. Switch roles.

Have each student write out step-by-step directions (a "program") of how to get to some particular place around the school (do not actually name the place). Students then exchange papers and try to reach the place in five minutes. When they return, have them explain the "bugs" in the program.

7. *A walking field trip.* Take your students on field trips to everything from the police department to the post office to the weather bureau to a local business using computerized information services. Many places that use computers may be within walking distance of the school. Have your children work out some good questions to ask.

8. *Junk sculpture.* Using a scavenger-hunt approach, have the students search out anything they can find that is related to or a product of computers—IBM care, library card, record album cover, receipt from automated teller, old transistor tubes from old radios, broken digital watch, universal product code on commercial item, etc.

9. *Art via the computer.* Computer networking gives students access to museum data banks all over the world. Using telephone lines and satellites, images can be brought into the classroom for students to analyze and change, leading toward creative production. If you don't have a good graphics program (or lack networking facilities) then some of these ideas can be carried out by simply bringing art forms into the classroom.

This activity is designed to help children appreciate how artists recreate a story through pictures. Children can become absorbed in the action of a picture. Entering into a picture, as they might a story dramatization, children can recognize how an artist uses lines to show movement and facial expression. They also can see how color is used to create mood and tone and how certain parts of a picture are highlighted.

10. *The want ads.* Bring in as many recent newspaper want ads as you can find. Have students bring in some as well. Have students see how many computer-related jobs they can find. You may even have them write make-believe resumés and letters responding to those ads and interview one another based on the want ads, resumés, and letters.

11. *Protecting people from computers.* Have the students ask adults they know about computer "mistakes" in their lives. Some students might even have examples of their own. Build a group language experience story. Connect it to articles on the same subject.

Following this activity, discuss how data banks work and privacy problems. Have the class come up with some "rules" for how computers should be used in our society.

12. *Does technology help or hurt?* Have students come up with a list of various technological breakthroughs and inventions and then list the pros and cons of each. Figure 7-1 shows an example.

From this activity students can see that every technological breakthrough usually has both positive and negative results. Questions like "What can it do that I haven't been able to do before?" and "Does it make our life more pleasant?" can be asked.

13. *Powerful tools have powerful effects.* Examine the mistakes of past predictions to look better at the future. Technology has a life of its own—it is ambiguous and difficult to predict. (Giving students a little ambiguity to deal with seems to help with future change.)

To make this point have students go over old newspaper and magazine files to find mistaken technological predictions. Put them up for everyone to see. For example, Edison thought that

FIGURE 7-1.

Invention	Pros	Cons
Automobile	freedom for indi-vidual rapid transportation could live further from work place	air pollution suburbs dependence on foreign energy source
Atomic energy		
Gene splicing		
Computers		
Television		
Telephones		
Airplanes		
Microwave ovens		

his phonograph would be used by the telegraph office to relay messages. Bell thought that his telephone would be used mainly by music lovers listening to distant concerts.

Discuss how in the late 1920s movies almost died with their

mouths shut. Color television was ready to be mass produced at that time; and, if the depression had not hit, "talkies" (thought to be a fad) would never have had the chance to get going.

Have the students make some future inferences about specific current technology. (For example, the use of protein rather than silicon for microchips. Will this be combined with gene-splitting to breed microscopic chips?)

14. *Networking.* See if you can communicate with other schools via a computer telecommunications network. You might even get a university computer center or private company to let you communicate with their computer. In California a number of businesses have encouraged schools to work out agreements with them. Students at several branches of California State University can, for example, access Lockheed's mainframe computer.

Chapter 8

Tapping into the World: Computer Telecommunications Networks and Schools

The first intelligent machines, the first computers, were involved in a very significant telecommunications system. German technicians during the late 1930s used the famous Enigma machine to encode their secret radio messages. In response, British scientists led by Alan Turing intercepted the radio messages and used the world's first electronic digital computer, the Colossus, to break the Germans' codes. Geopolitics and war preparations played a part in bringing together the first computerized telecommunications system. From their early stages of development, broadcast signals and electronic computers have had a symbiotic relationship—computers were used to code complex broadcast signals, and computers were used to interpret codes thought to be unbreakable.

Nearly 50 years later, schools are also finding it useful to combine computers and telecommunications, creating great educational potential across a broad spectrum of disciplines. Even schools that have just a few microcomputers have found that tapping into a database is an excellent way for many students to use a computer that may be available only periodically.

A microcomputer that operates independently within a classroom is indeed exciting; use the same microcomputer to communicate with other people, computers, and data bases, and dramatic things can happen. Quite simply, that's what computer telecommunications means: Communicating by long distance, using various combinations of computer and television technology. Or, computers talking to computers long distance. Computer telecommunication is more than this, however. Broadcast

127

signals plus computer capabilities are an example of synergy—the combination represents greater potential than either technology in isolation.

Recent developments in computer telecommunications have resulted in equipment capable of interactive text, graphics, speech, and video. Data bases now go beyond simple storage to manipulation and interactive transmission. By buying a communications software program and attaching a modem to your school microcomputer, you are ready to share information with just about any other personal computer, mainframe, or data base. Students can send messages, ask for help from a large audience, and communicate with less inhibition. Our major national libraries have now entered their books and periodicals into a computer, allowing us to use our personal computers to search for articles in a number of journals. In some fields it is even possible to instantly reproduce the entire text. People are linked to data in new combinations, and the potential applications within teaching and learning are intriguing.

COMPUTER TELECOMMUNICATIONS NETWORKS

When a group of computer users become involved in sending and receiving information, the system is often called a network. The general term *computer telecommunications network* refers to many different types of computer telecommunications systems. Some of these networks are operated on a national or even an international basis, while others are local systems. Some networks have general public access—all you need is the phone number and you can gain access to the system. Others are restricted, and only certain people are allowed to gain access to the system. The movie *War Games* depicted an example of someone illegally gaining access to a highly restricted network (a system run by the Pentagon).

If you have had no experience with computer telecommunications, you may wonder what the user actually does to hook up to a network. As described below, four components are necessary to become involved in computer telecommunications. Once these four components are in place, the user turns on the micro-computer, slides a diskette into the disk drive, and loads a program which directs the computer to send and receive information. With some communication programs, a brief menu appears at this point. The computer executes entry to the network through a series of messages sent across a telecommunications system. In some cases this is all done automatically by the computer and in other cases the user has to dial the telephone and give the computer instructions. A menu or table of contents often appears, and the user makes choices to send or receive desired information. Interaction is possible due to transmissions of computer data across a telecommunications system. With new digital compressers it is even possible to send pictoral images over standard telephone lines, giving us the potential to bring the resources of the outside world to our students in living color. They can even freeze these images on a screen and call up a text explanation.

NECESSARY COMPONENTS
FOR COMPUTER TELECOMMUNICATIONS

The four necessary components to use computer telecommunications follow.

Telecommunications Component

The most basic telecommunications component, next to the computer, is the MODEM. MODEM, short for MOdulator DEModulator, is a device that changes computer signals to signals that can be broadcast across some communications medium such as a telephone line. For example, computers can communicate with each other through a MODEM that fits on any standard telephone. You have to make sure that the modem on the computer that you are communicating with is set at the same speed as yours. The two common microcomputer speeds are 300 and 1200 baud. Fortunately some modems, like the Hayes Smartmodem, work at both 300 and 1200 baud. The computer impulses are translated into sound impulses, carried across phone lines, and then converted back into impulses a computer can recognize. Small computers and computer terminals can use telephone lines to tap into large mainframe systems and to communicate with other people using microcomputers. Most telephone lines today use twisted cable that is slow—30 characters per second—and takes up to a minute to transmit enough information to fill a microcomputer screen. Digital compressers help, but microwave and fiber optic telephone connections are much faster. Use of telephone lines in networking computers is usually convenient because nearly every home and workplace has a telephone. Very few classrooms, however, are presently wired for telephones. Telephone communication has its price—the cost of a long-distance call, use of a special telecommunications network, or subscription to a service that uses an 800 number.

Although telephone systems are the most common computer telecommunications link at present, many local area networks are connected directly with coaxial cable. The same information and images can also be sent among computers via satellite transmission, which makes computer networking much quicker and more spontaneous. It is possible to interface satellite communications with existing telephone and cable systems. National Public Radio (NPR) has cooperative agreements with several firms to use NPR's satellite system to transmit computer signals. This type of system could put the cost of computer telecommunications networks within reach for many schools.

Direct Broadcast Satellites (DBS)—to be taken into space by

the space shuttle in 1986—are powerful broadcast satellites that will transmit a signal that can be received by small personal dish antennae. These satellites can mean relatively inexpensive communication links in the future. Telephones could be bypassed altogether, and lengthy computer telecommunications hookups could become very affordable. Computer users may enjoy almost unlimited access to periodicals, libraries of software, bulletin boards, museum collections, and interactions with other people sitting at computer keyboards.

Computer Component

Networks of computers within a telecommunications system can include groups of microcomputers, groups of mainframe computers, and combinations of microcomputers and large computers. Enhancements and innovations put into all types of computers will have an effect on telecommunications capabilities. Memory size, operating systems, and communication capabilities of each machine are important factors within the network. Computer designers and engineers are paying increased attention to telecommunications—the latest models of personal computers allow for more complete and simpler communication with larger systems.

Software Component

Computers within a telecommunications network need programs (software) that direct the exchange of information among the computers. This software is called a *terminal program* or a *communications program.* One sophisticated communication program, Datacapture, directs the computer to record information received from a network source to a floppy disk at any time of the day (presumably when phone rates are lowest). The information on the diskette may then be read back into the computer and viewed at the user's convenience.

Television Component

Information transmitted to and from computers is most frequently displayed for the participants on a cathode-ray tube (CRT) or a television screen. The CRT, or television screen, can display text, graphics, and video images. High-definition digital television, a developing technology, provides many more pictorial bits of information and a larger screen than is currently used in most systems. This means that picture information can be tripled and image quality vastly improved for both small and large screen systems.

Some new computers are actually part of the TV. The Sharp X-1 is an example of a television set with a built-in computer and detachable keyboard (to control both). The set can be programmed to search for specific information, record programs, turn on or off, and switch channels at a certain time.

Not only can a computer present information it has received from a network visually; it can, with the appropriate equipment, present information aurally. Stereo television is another technological advancement that could be important for computer telecommunications. It is predicted that stereo television will capture more than 20 percent of the television market over the next several years. This means far better sound; and the sets have a built-in subchannel that allows listeners to choose a language other than English. Stereo television sets can also carry closed captions and mesh well with computers, videodisc players, video cassette recorders, and television teletext services.

COMPUTER TELECOMMUNICATIONS NETWORKS SERVE PEOPLE

People use computer telecommunications networks to do work, complete errands, take classes, and recreate. Government, business, individuals, special interest groups, and institutions are devising new ways in which to increase efficiency and capability with computer-based telecommunications systems.

Information Services

Electronic bulletin boards and electronic mail—two popular information services—provide convenient ways to communicate among computer users. In both cases, messages can be updated frequently and immediately disseminated to diverse locations. Mail and announcements "wait" for intended receivers and allow time for reflection and decision making.

Information utilities, another type of information service, involves access to a large collection of information stored in computers with very large memories. An example of an information utility is a hook-up with current New York Stock Exchange quotes and a personalized calculation of the status of the user's own portfolio. Another example is DIALOG, an encyclopedia data base that stores huge amounts of information on many subjects in a large computer. You tell the large computer what topic you want information on, and it transmits references and abstracts on that topic to your computer. DIALOG is like a giant library long distance.

One example of a national information service within education is SPECIALNET. This computer telecommunications system is a special education network that provides rapid communication among thousands of microcomputer users in 50 states and Canada. There are over 20 information bases that include educational programming, technology, and management areas with up-to-the-minute resources from experts in many fields. Services include electronic bulletin boards that display information on employment, federal legislation, conferences, curriculum practices, and computer software related to special education. The subscription cost is $200 per year plus a telephone fee that can range from $4–$18 per hour, depending on the time of day the network is used. There are also minor charges for storage time and copy services.

Wiring the Government

The Canadian Parliament is now using a telecommunications system called OASIS, that puts each member of Parliament in touch with a huge database. This network allows an MP to tap libraries of information, word processing equipment, their home riding, and even send electronic mail to other members. They can also use their microcomputer to call up color videos of prior speeches—their own or someone else's. Schools may be allowed to tap into some of the elements in the system.

Telecourses

Instructional units delivered through a broadcast medium are often called telecourses. It is not necessary to have computers involved in telecourses. Educational television is one example of a telecourse, and audio teleconferencing, using the regular telephone system, is another. The addition of computers to telecourses adds an important dimension—that of interaction among students and teachers. Some authorities (Baltzer, 1982; Sharples, 1982; Sweeney, 1983; Tucker, 1983) believe that telecourses will become more prevalent as educational institutions adapt their delivery systems to meet the needs of a diverse student population. Toffler (1980) writes of a future in which students will not travel from home to school but will receive instruction and submit lessons via a futuristic version of computer telecommunications networks.

Telecommuting

People who stay at home and use a combination of a telephone, a computer, and a television set as their link to the workplace are telecommuters, or teleworkers. Future teleworkers may never experience a traffic jam on the freeway at 7:30 a.m., and they will not necessarily have to live within driving distance of the company that employs them. Teleworking reduces the use of cars, saves time, has proven to increase productivity among clerical workers, and expands the labor pool to include those who must stay at home (especially the handicapped). Telecommuting is not a panacea. Eder (1983) points out that teleworkers may feel very isolated and could be cut off from creative interaction with colleagues. Because work is done in the home, family roles may be disrupted, and the pressure to work is present at all times. Employers and employees may find that some combination of teleworking and traditional commuting will be most productive and realistic.

Errands

Computer telecommunications networks can provide connections with all sorts of businesses, stores, and services. Individuals with computerized access to personal bank accounts, catalogs, and service menus find that running errands no longer takes large chunks of time—time that is better spent recreating or working. Shopping with the computer will not allow squeezing the fruit, but some people may find that the convenience outweighs the shortcomings. This type of service has been talked about by computer buffs for several years. It is about to be made available to the American public on a very serious level, however. Tom Shea (1984) reports that IBM, Sears, and CBS are working together to provide a service to households that will allow consumers to do their shopping, banking, and bill paying with their home and personal computers.

Recreation

Video game enthusiasts are finding that subscriptions to a network enable them to avoid the high costs of buying software that quickly becomes old hat and allow them to select from a large library of computer games. Some game subscription services are beginning to offer laser videodisc simulations. For example, some innovative technicians have superimposed a game grid over a real video of the space shuttle, allowing players to simulate an experience that only an elite group of astronauts and scientists have yet experienced.

Students Can Build Their Own Database

Recently I helped students in a middle school develop a database for themselves, and for sharing with others in diverse locations. We found it useful to use a software program ("Cornerstone" from Infocom, Inc., Cambridge, MA 02138) that was designed to help non-programmers develop databases. One of the information banks (utilities) the children created dealt with nutrition. After compiling data about a number of foods they did an analysis of their own vitamin and caloric intake. Another group of students built a large database around the concept of rock music, allowing other schools to use this tool to search for and acquire information.

COMPUTER TELECOMMUNICATIONS NETWORKS AND SCHOOLS

The technology of computer-controlled databases and telecommunications networks represents countless possible instructional and administrative applications.

While the technology of computer telecommunications is quite new and until very recently has been confined to computer buffs, schools are beginning to use computer telecommunications networks today, and plans for the future are being formed. "Learn Alaska," an instructional telecommunications network set up in 1980, provides a variety of services to communities throughout the state. In 1983, the Texas Board of Education established an advisory committee that will plan the development of a statewide information and telecommunications instructional system.

This section illustrates some of the activities schools are involved in and explores ways in which computer telecommunications networks can help and are helping educators to do their jobs.

Schools Serve Isolated Learners

Schools worldwide face some serious obstacles when the goal is to serve isolated learners. Some people never have experienced formal education because they never have had the opportunity to attend school. Computer telecommunications networks can play a part in serving geographically isolated individuals as well as individuals who are isolated because of a disability.

Geographic isolation. Computer telecommunications networks can upgrade educational opportunities for people living in rural areas and small communities. For example, a small rural school will have teachers who can teach most subjects well but may need help in a specialized area such as advanced math, computers, or a foreign language. In addition, schools with small student populations may have only a few students interested in specialized courses. A computer telecommunications network could deliver support in the form of instructional sessions, supplementary materials, and contact with a qualified teacher. In this way, education in a rural school need not be more limited than that provided in larger systems.

The province of Alberta has developed a program to help rural teachers network their computers for access to a central software library and technical support. The Universities of Lethbridge and Alberta even give their SPECIALNET number to isolated schools that want to tap into information from all over North America. In addition, the three major universities in the province will help schools upload and download information during times when telephone rates are least expensive.

Rural students may also receive telecourses in their homes, thus eliminating a great deal of travel which, in many rural areas, is hampered by rugged terrain and poor roads. The Rio

Saldo Community College in Arizona is currently using a variety of telecommunications delivery systems to make courses more accessible to students geographically isolated from the institution (Baltzer, 1982).

Isolation due to disability. It is difficult for many handicapped persons to leave home, get to a classroom, and return home. Transportation directors have tremendous problems getting physically handicapped students to special program sites, and children receiving homebound instruction may not get daily contact with a teacher. The situation becomes especially problematic with handicapped students in rural areas.

Some students experience a sense of isolation, even if they are able to physically attend classes; this is often the situation for deaf students. The TDD, or telecommunications device for the deaf, is a special application of a computer telecommunications network. In San Diego hearing impaired students use TDDs to send and receive private messages and general announcements (Pflaum, 1982). In the future, school personnel plan to present lessons using the TDD system and measure and graph individual student performance. Teachers feel that communication, language, and reading skills are all enhanced when their deaf students use the TDD system.

DEAFNET extends communication services to hearing-impaired individuals across the nation. This computer-based telecommunications network allows hearing-impaired people to communicate with deaf and hearing friends, classmates, and business acquaintances. Users of DEAFNET communicate on the network using teletype devices or computer terminals to send and receive messages. Conversations are immediate, or messages can be left and picked up as electronic mail. SRI of MENLO Park, California, is assisting deaf community leaders from the 20 largest cities in the United States in installing the network, organizing local user groups, and raising funds to expand and operate the services.

It is sometimes difficult for persons in rural areas and the handicapped to access specialists, experts, and resource persons. In addition, travel can be a particularly inefficient use of education monies and professional time. Interactive telecommunications systems may be very helpful to itinerant teachers, therapists, and school health workers in providing more contact time with isolated students. Personal visits remain important, but some type of network system offers the opportunity for frequent contact. Computer telecommunications networks allow geographically scattered teachers, learners, and support personnel to update and access records, assign lessons, submit work, and communicate about progress. This application of networking could bring currently isolated individuals into direct contact with everything the most privileged student might encounter.

Schools Teach Current Information

It is difficult to conceptualize how quickly knowledge in some fields is changing. Teachers and students often struggle to locate current, required information. This year's physics text may arrive in classrooms already partially outdated. Many school libraries are underfunded and unable to keep much of the collection current. Even when a school has access to the very latest periodical on a subject, the information may still be out of date. In some cases, the only way to give students the most updated information on a topic is to make an expert available to communicate with them directly.

Information services. Some schools may find that funds previously allocated for printed material may better be spent in subscriptions to computerized information services. Two existing data bases, CompuServe and The Source, offer a large number of services to subscribers, including several types of computer software that can be sent by telephone lines into a microcomputer. The services are accessed via a toll-free 800 telephone number; after an initial subscription fee, users are billed by the hour for the service and $5 per hour is an average fee. AT&T

also has several joint ventures (one with IBM) being readied for this year that will offer instant access to a number of data banks, including educational magazines.

The School Practices Information Network (SPIN), offered by Scott, Foresman and Company, gives subscribers access to over one million educational documents in nearly 20 data bases. Students and teachers have the opportunity to use this modern computer telecommunications network for everything from research projects to design of educational programs. SPIN's services include literature reviews, product information, job openings, and electronic mail. Schools can tap into SPIN by simply attaching a telephone to a computer, dialing an access number, and entering a password. The system may be used with Apple, Atari, TRS-80, Commodore PET, and IBM PC computers. The system will search thousands of citations in minutes and can provide specific information requested by the user. *Books in Print* and other information sources are updated weekly. There is a membership fee and a small charge for this service.

Specialized information services can be a tremendous tool for some teachers. For example, economic classes may subscribe to the Dow Jones Information Service (which has nearly 75,000 subscribers). The financial information includes the text of journals such as *Barton's* and *The Wall Street Journal.* Software is now available that will allow those hooked into the system to go from the economic world to the world of their own real or make-believe finances. For example, students can update and evaluate their own simulated accounts and make managerial-type decisions based on actual stock market quotes.

Access to experts. In computer telecommunications networks it is possible to have a printed and/or an aural presentation of an instructor's presentation transmitted to learners in different parts of the country. Not only will learners have access to experts in the field, but the technology can allow students to ask questions, receive highlighted notes, and transmit completed assignments. This type of network would bring some of the top authorities in a field in communication with a large number of students.

Computers can also be experts. Expert systems have moved out of the artificial intelligence laboratories at universities such as MIT and Stanford and are being applied in everything from locomotive repair to diagnosing disease to building other computers. An expert system builds a computer simulation model based on the skills of a human expert. The machine gets its knowledge and intelligence from a human counterpart. Prediction, decision making, problem solving, and other forms of specific expertise are programmed into the computer.

When expert systems are part of a computer network, classroom computers can tap into the stored memories of top world experts that have been stored in the computer data base. In addition to this, software programs have been developed that will enable the teacher (with no programming background) to develop a very specific local expert system by allowing the teacher to fill in some data and letting the machine build up the knowledge itself. For example, KES software at Arlington, Virginia, is about to market a program that will allow the user to build his or her own expert system.

Computer telecommunications is also playing a role at the university level. The National University Teleconference Network has over one hundred institutions participating—from San Diego State University to Dartmouth. When the expense of telecourses is spread over a large number of colleges, the cost diminishes dramatically. In fact, just about every campus can afford to put together at least a receiving system. The network currently charges $2,000 to join and will assist campuses in organizing telecourses.

Schools Present Quality Learning Experiences

Educators are constantly striving to present quality learning experiences that are motivating, relevant, and effective. A technology that will allow video images from far off places to come into the classroom and allow students to react, manipulate, and transmit their own information certainly has the potential to provide quality learning experiences. During 1983 and 1984 a number of learning networks have begun, geared primarily for adult learners. Telelearning, a company based in San Francisco, combines computers and live instructors to teach nearly 200 educational courses via their computer telecommunications network. To use the system a student must have access to a computer with at least 64K of memory (available on most classroom computers) and a MODEM for telephone lines.

Electronic field trips. Imagine a field trip in which a class of fourth graders could visit a site hundreds of miles from their school building and still make it back in time for lunch. With electronic field trips, in fact, students never physically leave the classroom, yet they can be exposed to countless real-life events and people. Of course, such electronic traveling is limited to locations with appropriate and compatible equipment.

Baltimore public school students in Spanish classes are practicing their skills with Spanish-speaking policemen, actors, bankers, artists, and scientists in Miami. The signal is sent 22,300 miles up to the Westar 4 satellite and picked up by satellite dishes in both Baltimore and Miami. In the future, the Baltimore School District plans to put its students in touch with people in Costa Rica and Spain.

A Fusion of Television, Computers, and Print

Microcomputers and television are technologies that have complementary educational potential. Bank Street College's *The Voyage of the Mimi* and the Agency for Instructional Television's *Solutions Unlimited* broadcast weekly educational TV/computer programs. These televised lessons (also available for VCRs) connect to computer software and print materials. All you need for classroom use is a television set, microcomputer, and some ability to read print. Computer networks combined with educational television provides teachers with a variety of opportunities, including access to up-to-date, broadcast related, curriculum materials. Computer linked networks of classrooms can also work together on projects based on television programs.

New ways of thinking. When we can communicate with an extremely powerful computer, the tutorial possibilities are endless. Students can be brought to a vast warehouse of knowledge. The future holds the possibility for a richness in learning experiences by combining emotional, perceptual, and motivational factors with modern technology. The struggle between idea and image—seeing the relationship between colors and shapes—opens paths from which we can both view a new universe and see our present one differently.

As far as schools are concerned, technological competency is a process of helping students to become aware of and learn to use the collection of tools developed for different subjects. Such competency involves being able to use a computer as a research tool in a particular field or being able to use different telecommunications configurations to solve problems in different ways. Applications need not be limited to the sciences, but may also include the arts. Music students may access vast information banks of visual music and transmit pieces consisting of both melody and movement. Computer telecommunications networks allow computers to learn from each other and from people. In turn, we can increase our spatial understanding and learning from both computers and other people.

Software banks. Computer telecommunications networks can potentially solve software purchasing problems for large school districts. When school systems must buy numerous copies of a piece of instructional software, a large investment is going into a single instructional program. Teachers may use the program for a few weeks and then put it away for next year's group of students. At the same time, a teacher in another building may need a piece of software that exists somewhere within the district, but there is no efficient way of getting the software from place to place.

Software banks—large collections of instructional and managerial programs that are put onto a telecommunications network—can be a tremendous help to teachers as they design individualized educational programs for their students. Software banks may also represent a very cost-effective way for districts to make instructional software available to all computer users within the system. Although copyright regulations are a concern, the International Council for Computers in Education (ICCE) has articulated a policy that will protect both authors and publishers and allow schools to share software via networks (Judd, 1984).

Schools Provide Staff Development

There doesn't seem to be a general model for staff development in computer based technology. But certain evolving combinations of software, hardware, curriculum, and teacher training are likely to be effective in different contexts.

In-service training for teachers is notorious for being inconvenient and ineffective, yet teachers and staff need to update their skills and learn new techniques. Computer telecommunications networks could contribute toward making personalized in-service programs available at the convenience of the individual faculty or staff member. Having teachers take the lead in using this new technology for their own professional development will also help educate them on the latest instructional possibilities in using computer telecommunications networking with their own students. In this way educators can meet professional training needs in many areas and model the use of the latest technology.

Schools Administer Large Groups of People

Using computers to manage school records, budgets, and inventory is nothing new. The added dimension of telecommunications can make gathering and analyzing all sorts of information more efficient. Schools may find themselves looking to successful businesses for models of telecommunications applications in management and decision making. Electronic mail and computer bulletin boards may be just a few of the many ways in which administrators will routinely use computer telecommunications networks.

Computer networks can also be used to link several school districts when they have a common administrative problem. School districts in south Florida participate in a computer network that contains school records for children of migrant farm workers. By transmitting a child's current assessment and achievement data, teachers are saving valuable instructional time that in the past had to be spent determining a child's current level of skills. This is but one example of how school districts may combine resources to help better serve their students.

CAVEATS AND THORNY PROBLEMS

Computer telecommunications technology, in several forms, will become a widely used tool within education. Educators will be the ones called upon to incorporate computer-based networking and telecommunications in the mainstream of instruction and administration. Their decisions need to be based on a thorough knowledge of the technological capabilities and, most importantly, on the characteristics of effective instruction.

Cost

With tight budgets and expanding roles, schools are sometimes reluctant to make major investments in new technologies. The cost of computer telecommunications networks may simply be beyond what many districts can realistically afford. The Baltimore School District, for example, estimated that they would have had to pay nearly $3,000 for the electronic field trip their students took to Miami. The trip was made affordable because the telephone company donated a line and the University of Maryland loaned the use of a satellite receiver dish.

Although costs are decreasing, many schools still find it prohibitive to link computers with any sort of telecommunications system. The danger is that the "have nots" will become increasingly isolated. Districts with money and contacts will benefit from the technology—less affluent schools will not. Tucker (1983) sees great promise in the educational application of telecommunications but observes that funding for such systems is a low-priority item.

Planning

There are some things that computer telecommunications systems can do quite well; there are just as many cases in which use of these complex systems is more flash than function. Effective uses of computer telecommunications networks will reflect careful planning and appropriate application. Sweeney (1983) provides a framework for successful educational applications of telecommunications: (a) gain the support of administrative personnel, (b) form an advisory committee, (c) designate personnel for designing the program and the technical aspects of the systems, (d) devise effective operating procedures, (e) be sure that the equipment matches the goals of the program, (f) consider both one-time and ongoing costs, and (g) implement both formative evaluation and cost analysis.

Planning for computer telecommunications networks involves an awareness of the technological potential and sound instructional design. At present, there is little available information as to the effectiveness of such systems. Schools that do implement telecommunications networks should make efforts to share data related to costs and results with other educators.

Privacy

Computer pirates may be on their way to becoming future folk heroes, but the potential for piracy is a very real concern for any group using computer telecommunications networks. Administrators who choose to enter student records on a network system will also have to institute safeguards to protect those records. School systems that subscribe to information services and software banks may have to take steps to ensure that unauthorized persons are not also using the system. Schools may find themselves in consultation with legal authorities to define both risks and responsibilities in the area of privacy and computer networks.

SUMMARY

In helping educators become aware of the learning and managerial potential of computer telecommunications networks, it is important to see how the present technology has grown out of the past, what services are now available, and what will be on-line in the future. Computer telecommunications networks are a significant part of our technology-oriented society.

Computer telecommunications networks can help students go beyond a narrow range of academic skills and exercise the full range of intellectual and physical capacities—artistic, logical, linguistic, musical, and spatial. The latest computer telecommunications networking technology does have the potential for helping schools make a positive difference in the lives of students, but such a goal will not be met without cost, risk, and error. The promise for the future is there, but we must take purposeful steps to make it happen for ourselves and for our students. Figure 8-1 summarizes opportunities in telecommunications.

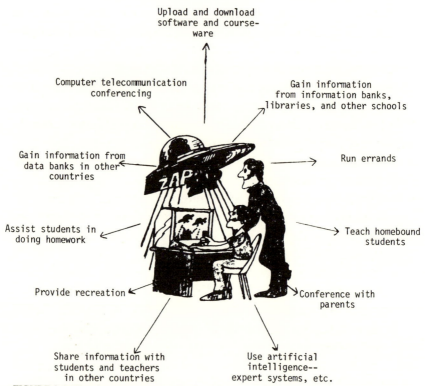

Upload and download
software and course-
ware

Computer telecommunication
conferencing

Gain information
from information banks,
libraries, and other schools

Gain information from
data banks in other
countries

Run errands

Assist students in
doing homework

Teach homebound
students

Provide recreation

Conference with
parents

Share information with
students and teachers
in other countries

Use artificial
intelligence--
expert systems, etc.

FIGURE 8-1. The classroom microcomputer can be used in telecommunications to enhance the educational process in the above ways.

EXAMPLES OF GENERAL INFORMATION SYSTEMS

Most of these systems can be accessed through TeleNet which is less expensive than some direct phone calls.

Computer Telecommunications System: CompuServe
Type: Information service with electronic mail, CB simulation, and hundreds of options.
Intended Audience: General audience.
Description: Offers a wide variety of services:
News, weather, and sports
Finance including information on stocks, bonds, and mutual funds

Entertainment with theater, book, movie, and restaurant reviews; travel information (e.g., airline guides) and you can even book a trip

Communications and special interest groups

Home which includes the World Book Encyclopedia on-line; electronic shopping and banking; home educational programs; information on food preparation, child care, health; a real potpourri of information

Personal computing with games, software exchange, programming languages

Cost: One time membership fee of approximately $25. (Fee differs from area to area.) On-line fee varied with baud rate and time of day; for 300 baud, day fee is $22.50 per hour; evening fee is $5 per hour.

For further information: Sign-up kit can be purchased at local Radio Shack dealers (which puts you on the system in two hours) or write CompuServe, 5000 Arlington Center Boulevard, P.O. Box 20212, Columbus, OH 43220; (614) 457-8600.

How to Get the Most Out of CompuServe, C. Bowen & D. Peyton, Bantam Books, New York, NY, 278 pp, $12.95 (1984). This book about the CompuServe Information Service shows how to get what you need without practice time and without running up huge user fees. Included are an on-line tour of the information service including logging in; passwords and handles; CompuServe menus and how to use them; how to use electronic mail; using the conference channels; CompuServe etiquette; special interest groups; free programs; accessing news, weather, stock quotes, and games; and how to improve the system. The book also has a survival kit, including an electronic address book for major service.

Computer Telecommunications System: The Source
Intended Audience: General audience

Description: Offers a wide variety of services:
  Communications
  Business including financial markets, commodities, portfolio
    management
  Consumer services such as shopping, travel, personal finance
  Entertainment including games, horoscopes
  Personal publishing
  Travel, air schedules, restaurant and hotel guides
  Educational drill programs
  Computational programs for statistics, finance, engineering
  UPI news, sports, and reference
Cost: One time membership fee of approximately $100. Month-
    ly minimum fee of $9 (even if you don't use it). On-line fee
    varies by baud rate and time of day: for 300 baud, day fee is
    $20.75 per hour, evening fee is $7.74 per hour.
For Further Information: The Source, 1616 Anderson Road,
    McLean, VA 22102; (703) 734-7500.

EXAMPLES OF BIBLIOGRAPHIC DATA BASES

Cave paintings could probably be considered the first databases. The computer, and related telecommunication devices,
has resulted in a tremendous amplification of our ability to collect and manipulate data over great distances. Information stored
in these data banks (utilities) are non-diminishing when people
pull out information—unlike traditional libraries, where when
all the books on a subject are borrowed there are no more
resources until they are returned.

The following are easy systems to use and offer novices help
in search strategies.

Computer Telecommunications System: Knowledge index
Type: On-line searching of professional data bases
Intended Audience: Educators and other professionals

Description: Evening access on weekdays, all day on weekends.
Offers a wide variety of data bases:
Agriculture
Books
Business information
Computers and electronics—includes International Software Database, Microcomputer Index, and Computer Database. This allows you to say, for example, "I want to see what is out there for simulations of nuclear power," and back comes the information.
Corporate news
Education—includes ERIC
Engineering
Government publications
Magazines
Medicine—includes MEDLINE
News
Psychology—includes PSYCINFO
Cost: One time membership fee of approximately $40. On-line fee of $24 per hour. Articles can be ordered for fee plus price of photocopy.
For Further Information: Knowledge Index, DIALOG Information Services, Inc., 3460 Hillview Avenue, Palo Alto, CA 94304.

Computer Telecommunications System: BRS/After Dark
Type: On-line searching of professional data bases
Intended Audience: Educators and other professionals
Description: Evening access on weekdays, all day on weekends.
Offers a wide variety of data bases:
Science/medicine
Business/financial
Reference—includes ERIC, Exceptional Child Education Resources, Bilingual Education Bibliographic Abstracts, and School Practices Information File

Social sciences/humanities—includes National Information Sources on the Handicapped, National Rehabilitation Information Center, Psych INFO
Cost: One time membership fee of approximately $50. Monthly minimum fee of $12. On-line fee varies by data base: e.g., ERIC costs $6 per hour.
For Further Information: BRS, 1200 Route 7, Latham, NY 12110.

"Infoglobe" is an example of another large scale database. It is in Canada and contains, among other things, the complete text of Toronto's "Globe and Mail" newspaper as far back as 1977.

EXAMPLES OF EDUCATIONAL
BULLETIN BOARD SYSTEMS

There are thousands of electronic bulletin boards that range from children's messages to teenlines to X-rated dating services.

Computer Telecommunications System: SpecialNet
Type: Bulletin board system with electronic mail service
Intended Audience: Special educators
Description: Offers over 25 topical bulletin boards:

ASSESSMENT	EXCHANGE
ASSISTIVE DEVICE	FEDERAL
CEC NEWS	GIFTED
CHAIN (for parents)	LITIGATION
COMPUTER	MULTIHANDI-
CONFERENCE	CAPPED
	OPINION
CONGRESS	POLICY
CONSULTANT	PRACTICES
CSPD	RFP

DEAFNESS	RURAL
EARLY CHILDHOOD	SLATE
EDUTECH	TELEVISION
EMPLOYMENT	VISION

A clock board will allow you to up load and down load information automatically, at midnight for example, when the phone rates are lowest. All you need to do is put in the diskette at the end of the day and it will go on by itself.

The EXCHANGE board allows users to ask questions and respond to the questions of others.

CSPD (Comprehensive System of Personnel Development) provides information about training of special educators; PRACTICES describes effective programs for classroom instruction, teacher training, and administration; RFP lists requests for proposals; and SLATE assists state-level policy-makers with information about technology.

Cost: Subscription fee of $200 per year. On-line fee of $4 to $23 per hour depending on time of day. *Education Daily* is available for additional yearly charge.

For Further Information: SpecialNet, National Association of State Directors of Special Education, 1201 16th Street, NW, Suite 404E, Washington, DC 20036; (202) 822-7933. There are system operators who will help you through any problems.

EXAMPLES OF FREE EDUCATIONAL BULLETIN BOARDS

These can be provided by everything from computer stores to universities.

Educational Technology PMS (People's Message Service), sponsored by the San Diego State University Department of Educational Technology; computer access phone is (619)

265-3428. The purpose is to allow educators to communicate about microcomputer telecommunications technology. Only one phone line is available so it may take some time to get in.

Handicapped Educational Exchange (HEX), c/o Richard Barth, 11523 Charlton Drive, Silver Spring, MD 20902; computer access phone is (301) 593-7033.

Living Bulletin Board System for Educators, sponsored by Computer- Using Educators and the Far West Regional Educational Laboratory; computer access phone is (415) 565-3037.

Notre Dame Bulletin Board System, "The Leprechaun"; computer access phone is (219) 239-5875.

RESOURCES FOR FURTHER INFORMATION

These selected references are a partial list that has been found to be of value to teachers who are new telecommunicators.

Basic Information about Telecommunication

Archibald, D. (1983). Apple on the phone: What is and what's to come in telecommunications. *Softtalk, 3*(5), 184-190. [Explains how telecommunication works, defines common terms]

Barden, W. (1983). Talking in tones. *Popular Computing, 3*(2), 65-67. [Explains how modems work]

Keogh, J. (1983). Dialing for data. *Personal Software, 1*(2), 36-49. [Buyer's guide to modems and terminal programs]

Descriptions of Electronic Data Banks and Information Systems

Edwards, M. D. (1983). Plugging into the nation's corkboards. *TLC, 1*(2), 66-70. [Information for educators about electronic bulletin boards]

Emmett, A. (1983). Electronic bulletin boards. *Personal*

Computing, 7(6), 64-69. [Explains what electronic bulletin boards do and how to set one up using commercial software]
Neumann, R. (1982). Data banks: Opening the door to a world of information. *Electronic Learning, 2*(3), 56-61. [Overview of telecommunications, a directory of data banks, and a buyer's guide for modems]
Rubin, C. (1984). Touring the on-line data bases. *Personal Computing, 8*(1), 82-95, 196. [Describes general information systems such as CompuServe, Dow Jones News/Retrieval, and The Source]
Zarley, C. (1983). Dialing into data bases. *Personal Computing, 7* (12), 135-139. [Overview of bibliographic retrieval systems such as DIALOG, ORBIT, and BRS]

Descriptions of Electronic Communication Systems

Cross, T. B. (1982). Tele/conferencing: The new school tool. *Educational Computer, 2*(6), 25-26.
Kurland, N. D. (1983). Have computer, will not travel: Meeting electronically. *Phi Delta Kappan, 65,* 124-126.
Strehlo, K. (1983). Mail call, mail call! *Personal Computing, 7*(12), 126-133. [An introduction to electronic mail]

Information About Special Education Applications in Telecommunication

Campbell, R., & Walsh, S. (1982). Computer assisted telecommunications: SpecialNet, an expanding resource. *Journal of Special Education Technology, 5*(4), 65-68.

REFERENCES

Adams, D. M.; Bott, D. (1984). Tapping into the world: Computer telecommunication networks and schools. *Computers in the Schools, 3.*
Adams, D. M.; Fuchs, M. (1985). AI for ESL. *Tech Trends, 30*(3), April, 30-31.
Adams, D. M.; Fuchs, M. (1985). New digitized literacies: Mixing visual media, the arts, print and computer-based technology. *Educational Technology,* May.

Adams, D. M.; Fuchs, M. (1985). Meet the middle management micro. *American School and University,* April, 51-54.

Adams, D. M.; Fuchs, M. (1985). Making something happen for Hispanic students: Using some of the first practical application programs from artificial intelligence research. *Microcomputers in Education, 5*(4), 1-10.

Hunter, B. *My students use computers: Learning activities for computer literacy.* New Jersey: Prentice-Hall, 1983.

Eder, P. F. (1983). Telecommuters: The stay-at-home work force of the future. *The Futurist, 17*(3), 30-32, 34-35.

Judd, R. C. (1984). Networks for education. *Educational Computer, 4*(1), 18-19, 47.

Pflaum, M. E. (1982). The California connection: Interfacing a telecommunications device for the deaf (TDD) and an Apple computer. *American Annals for the Deaf,* 127, 573-584.

Sharples, M. (1982). Educational technology and the open university. *Teaching at a Distance, 22,* 15-20.

Shea. T. (1984). Big firms team up on videotex project. *Infoworld, 6*(11), 13.

Stone, M. D. *Getting on-line: A guide to accessing computer information services.* New Jersey: Prentice-Hall, 1984.

Sweeney, J. F. (1983). Implementing teleconferencing educational programming in a community college consortium. *Community Services Catalyst, 13,* 10-13.

Tucker, M. S. (1983). The turning point: Telecommunications and higher education. *Journal of Communication, 33*(1), 118-130.

Resources

EDUCATIONAL COMPUTING JOURNALS

AEDS MONITOR, Association for Educational Data Systems, 1201 Sixteenth Street, NW, Washington, DC 20036.

CLASSROOM COMPUTER NEWS, Intentional Educators, Inc., 51 Spring Street, Watertown, MA 02172, (617) 923-7707.

COMPUTERS IN THE SCHOOLS, Haworth Press, Inc., 28 East 22nd Street, New York, NY 10010.

COMPUTERS, READING AND LANGUAGE ARTS, PO Box 13247, Oakland, CA 94661, (415) 339-1106.

THE COMPUTING TEACHER, Department of Computer and Information Sciences, University of Oregon, Eugene, OR 97403, (503) 689-4414.

EDUCATIONAL COMPUTING, MAGSUB (Subscription Services), Ltd., Oakfield House, Perrymount Road, Haywards Heath, Sussex RH 16 3DH, England.

EDUCATIONAL TECHNOLOGY, 140 Sylvan Avenue, Englewood Cliffs, NJ 07632, (201) 871-4007.

ELECTRONIC EDUCATION, Communications, Inc., Suite 220, 1311 Executive Center Drive, Tallahassee, FL 32301, (904) 878-4178.

ELECTRONIC LEARNING, Scholastic, Inc., 902 Sylvan Avenue, Box 2001, Englewood Cliffs, NJ 07632, (201) 567-7900.

JOURNAL OF COMPUTER-BASED INSTRUCTION, AD-CIS, Computer Center, Western Washington University, Bellingham, WA 98225.

JOURNAL OF EDUCATIONAL TECHNOLOGY SYSTEMS, Baywood Publishing Company, Inc., 120 Marine Street, Box D, Farmingdale, NY 11735, (516) 249-7130.

157

MICROCOMPUTERS IN EDUCATION, Chapel Hill Drive, Fairfield, CT 06432.
MICRO-SCOPE, JEM Research, Discovery Park, University of Victoria, Box 1700, Victoria B.C. V8W 2Y2, Canada.
T.H.E. JOURNAL, PO Box 992, Acton, MA 01720, (617) 263-3607.

GENERAL COMPUTING PERIODICALS

BYTE, 70 Main Street, Peterborough, NH 03458, (603) 924-9281.
CREATIVE COMPUTING, PO Box 789-M, Morristown, NJ 07960, (800) 631-8112 and (210) 540-0445.
KILOBAUD MICROCOMPUTING, Subscription Department, PO Box 997, Farmingdale, NY 11737.
PERSONAL COMPUTER WORLD, c/o Steve England, 41 Rathbone Place, London W1P 1DE, England, (01) 637-7991.
PERSONAL COMPUTING, PO Box 1408, Riverton, NJ 08077.
POPULAR COMPUTING, 70 Main Street, Peterborough, NH 03458, (603) 924-9281.

SOURCES OF CRITICAL REVIEWS
OF EDUCATIONAL SOFTWARE

AMERICAN MICRO MEDIA, Box 306, Red Hood, NY 12571, (914) 756-2557.
BOOKLIST, 50 East Huron Street, Chicago, IL 60611.
COMPUTERS IN THE SCHOOLS, The Haworth Press, Inc., 28 East 22nd Street, New York, NY 10010.
THE BOOK REPORT, Box 14466, Columbus, OH 43214.
COURSEWARE REPORT CARD, 150 West Carob Street, Compton, CA 90220.
DIGEST OF SOFTWARE REVIEWS: EDUCATION, 1341 Bulldog Lane, Suite C, Fresno, CA 93710.

EPIE MICRO-COURSEWARE, PRO/FILES, EPIE & Consumers Union, Box 620, Stony Brook, NY 11790.

JEM REFERENCE MANUAL, JEM Research, Discovery Park, University of Victoria, Box 1700, Victoria, B.C. V8W 2Y2, Canada.

JOURNAL OF APPLE COURSEWARE REVIEW, Apple Computer, Inc., Box 28426, San Jose, CA 95159.

MICRO MEDIA REVIEW, Box 125, Ridgefield, CT 06877.

MICROSIFT REVIEWS, Northwest Regional Laboratory, 300 SW Sixth Avenue, Portland, OR 97204.

EDUCATIONAL JOURNALS THAT CARRY OCCASIONAL ARTICLES ON COMPUTING

ARITHMETIC TEACHER, CURRICULUM REVIEW, 517 South Jefferson Street, Chicago, IL 60607.

EDUCATIONAL TECHNOLOGY, 140 Sylvan Avenue, Englewood Cliffs, NJ 07632.

EPIE REPORT, Epie Institute, Box 620, Stony Brook, NY 11790.

INSTRUCTOR, 7 Bank Street, Dansville, NY 14437.

JOURNAL OF LEARNING DISABILITIES, 5615 West Cermak Road, Cicero, IL 60650.

LEARNING MAGAZINE, 530 University Avenue, Palo Alto, CA 94301.

MATHEMATICS TEACHER, National Council of Teachers of Mathematics, 1906 Association Drive, Reston, VA 22091.

MEDIA AND METHODS, 1511 Walnut Street, Philadelphia, PA 19102.

NEWSLETTERS FROM COMPUTER USERS' GROUPS

ATARI COMPUTER ENTHUSIASTS (Atari), 3662 Vine Maple Drive, Eugene, OR 97405.

CHICATRUG NEWS (TRS-80), Chicago TRS-80 Users Group, 203 North Wagash, Room 1510, Chicago, IL 60601.

CUE NEWSLETTER, Computer-Using Educators, Box 18547, San Jose, CA 95158.

MACUL JOURNAL, Michigan Association for Computer Users in Learning, 33500 Van Born Road, Wayne, MI 48184.

MIDNIGHT SOFTWARE GAZETTE (PET), Central Illinois PET Users' Group, 635 Maple Court, Mt. Zion, IL 62549.

USERS: THE MECC INSTRUCTIONAL COMPUTING NEWSLETTER, 2520 North Broadway Drive, St. Paul, MN 55113.

COMPUTER JOURNALS THAT CARRY OCCASIONAL ARTICLES ON EDUCATION

BYTE, 70 Main Street, Peterborough, NH 03458, (603) 924-9281.

COMPUTE! Box 5406, Greensboro, NC 27403.

CREATIVE COMPUTING, Box 780-M, Morristown, NJ 07690.

80 MICROCOMPUTING (TRS-80), 80 Pine Street, Peterborough, NH 03458.

80 SOFTWARE CRITIQUE (TRS-80), Box 134, Waukegan, IL 60085.

INFOWORLD, 375 Cochituate Road, Box 800, Framington, MA 01701.

INTERFACE AGE, 16704 Marquardt Avenue, Cerritos, CA 90701.

INTERNATIONAL APPLE CORE, 908 George Street, Santa Clara, CA 95050.

MICROCOMPUTING, 80 Pine Street, Peterborough, NH 03458.

NIBBLE (Apple), Box 325, Lincoln, MA 01773.

PEELINGS II (Apple), 945 Brook Circle, Las Cruces, NM 88001.

PERSONAL COMPUTER AGE (IBM), 10057 Commercial Avenue, Tujunga, CA 91042.

PERSONAL COMPUTING, 50 Essex Street, Rochelle Park, NJ 07662.

POPULAR COMPUTING, 70 Main Street, Peterborough, NH 03458.

SOFTSIDE, Box 68, Milford, NH 03055.

SOFTALK MAGAZINE (Apple), 11021 Magnolia Boulevard, North Hollywood, CA 91601.

SOME BOOKS IN EDUCATIONAL COMPUTING

Ahuja, Vijay, *Design and Analysis of Computer Communication Networks,* McGraw-Hill, 1982.

Antebi, Elizabeth, *The Electronic Epoch,* Van Nostrand Reinhold Company, 1983.

Barr, Avron, *The Handbook of Artificial Intelligence,* William Kaufman, 1981.

Bitter, Gary G., *Computers in Today's World,* John Wiley & Sons, 1984.

Book of IBM Software, Addison-Wesley Publishing, 1984.

Brand, Stewart (Ed.). *Whole Earth Software Catalog,* Quantum/Doubleday, 1984.

Ciacia, Steve, *Build Your Own Z-80 Computer,* Byte Books, 1979.

Cherry, George W., *Pascal Programming Structures: An Introduction to Systematic Programming,* Reston Publishing Co., 1980.

Christie, L., & Christie, J., *The Encyclopedia of Microcomputer Terminology,* Prentice-Hall, Inc., 1984.

Collected Essays on Computing, Digital Press, 1980.

Daiute, Colette, *Writing & Computers,* Addison-Wesley, 1985.

Evans, Christopher, *The Micro Millennium,* Washington Square Press/Pocketbook Publications, 1981.

Frank, Mary (Ed.), *Young Children in a Computerized Environment,* The Haworth Press, 1982.

Fox, Joseph M., *Software and Its Development,* Prentice-Hall, 1982.

Futrell, M., & Geisert, P., *The Well-Trained Computer,* Educational Technology Publications, 1984.

Glassner, Andrew S., *Computer Graphics User's Guide,* Bobbs-Merrill Educational Pub., 1984.

Guide to Personal Computing, Digital Press, 1982.

Hanson, Owen, *Design of Computer Data Files,* Computer Science Press, 1982.

Klingman, Edwin E., *Microprocessor Systems Design,* Vol. II, Prentice-Hall, 1982.

Lathrop, Ann, & Goodson, Bobby, *Courseware in the Classroom,* Addison-Wesley, 1983.

Leggett, Stanton (Ed.), *Microcomputers Go to School,* Teach'Em, Inc., 1984.

Libes, Sol, *Fundamentals and Application of Digital Logic Circuits,* Hayden Book Company, 1980.

Marroquin, Raul, *The Link: Juan Maranas Political Campaign,* Maastricht Holland, 1982.

Mateosian, Richard, *Inside BASIC Games,* Sybex, 1981.

Math, Irwin, *Bits and Pieces,* Scribner Book Companies, Inc., 1984.

Micro Data Base Systems, Inc., *Discovering Knowledge Man,* Howard W. Sams & Co., 1984.

Mitchell, Joyce Slayton, *Your Job in the Computer Age,* Scribner Book Companies, Inc., 1984.

Papert, Seymour, *Mindstorms: Children, Computers and Powerful Ideas,* Basic Books, 1980.

Pasadena Technology Press, *Lee's Guide to Published Computer Programs,* 1984.

Pattis, Richard E., *Karel the Robot,* Wiley & Sons, 1981.

Peterson, Dale, *Big Things from Little Computers: A Layperson's Guide to Personal Computing,* Prentice-Hall, 1982.

Pitts, Gerald N., & Bateman, Barry L., *Essentials of COBOL Programming: A Structured Approach,* Computer Science Press, 1982.

Rappaport, Irwin, *Textedit,* Wayne Green Books, 1982.

Safford, Edward L., Jr., *The Complete Handbook of Robotics,* TAB Books, 1980.

Sigel, E., & Giglio, L., *Guide to Software Publishing,* Knowledge Industry Publications, Inc., 1984.

Simon, Herbert, *The Sciences of the Artificial* (2nd Ed.), MIT Press, 1981.

Sommer, Elyse, *Perfect Writer Made Perfectly Clear,* Chilton Book Company, 1984.

Spangenburg, R., & Moser, D., Personal Word Processing, Wadsworth Publishing Company, 1984.

Speitel, Tom et al., *Science Computer Programs for Kids and Other People,* Reston Publishing Company, 1984.

Spencer, Donald, *Exploring the World of Computers,* Camelot Publishing Company, 1982.

Spencer, Donald, *Computer Dictionary for Everyone,* Scribner Book Companies, Inc., 1984.

Willen, David C., *BASIC Programming with the IBM PCjr,* Howard Sams & Company, Inc., 1984.

Willis, Jerry, & Johnson, D. LaMont, *Computers Teaching and Learning,* dilithium Press, 1983.